How Far We Slaves Have Come!

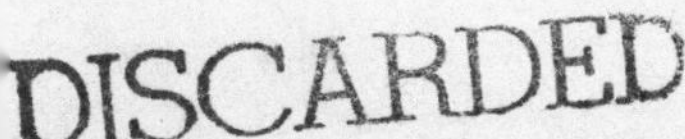

NELSON MANDELA
FIDEL CASTRO

HOW FAR WE SLAVES HAVE COME!

South Africa and Cuba in Today's World

PATHFINDER
New York London Montreal Sydney

ISBN 0-87348-729-X paper; ISBN 0-87348-497-5 cloth
Library of Congress Catalog Card Number 91-66760
Manufactured in the United States of America

First edition, 1991
Second printing, 1993

Cover and book design: Toni Gorton
Cover photo: Mary-Alice Waters

Pathfinder
410 West Street, New York, NY 10014, U.S.A.
Fax: (212) 727-0150

Pathfinder distributors around the world:
Australia (and Asia and the Pacific):
Pathfinder, 19 Terry St., Surry Hills, Sydney, N.S.W. 2010
Britain (and Europe, Africa except South Africa, and Middle East):
Pathfinder, 47 The Cut, London, SE1 8LL
Canada:
Pathfinder, 6566, boul. St-Laurent, Montreal, Quebec, H2S 3C6
Iceland:
Pathfinder, Klapparstíg 26, 2d floor, 121 Reykjavík
New Zealand:
Pathfinder, La Gonda Arcade, 203 Karangahape Road, Auckland
Postal address: P.O. Box 8730, Auckland
Sweden:
Pathfinder, Vikingagatan 10, S-113 42, Stockholm
United States (and Caribbean, Latin America, and South Africa):
Pathfinder, 410 West Street, New York, NY 10014

CONTENTS

Top: July 26, 1991, rally in Matanzas, Cuba. (Photo: Mary-Alice Waters/*Militant*)

PREFACE

On July 26, 1991, Nelson Mandela, president of the African National Congress (ANC), and Fidel Castro, president of Cuba, spoke together for the first time on the same platform. On this historic occasion, they were addressing a rally of tens of thousands in Matanzas, Cuba, marking the thirty-eighth anniversary of the opening of the Cuban revolution.

The pages that follow contain the complete text of the speeches by Nelson Mandela and Fidel Castro at the Matanzas rally, as well as the resolution of Cuba's Council of State awarding Mandela the José Martí medal, the highest honor conferred by the government of Cuba. Here Mandela and Castro explain why the two struggles of which they are central leaders—the battle to build a revolutionary democratic movement in South Africa capable of uprooting the apartheid system and the battle to strengthen the internationalism and communist direction of the Cuban revolution—have been closely intertwined for the past three decades. Through their words, we can better understand why the struggles being waged by the working people of South Africa and Cuba are today the most important examples for fighters everywhere who want to rid the earth of racism and exploitation and chart a road forward for all humanity.

In November 1975 the Cuban government, in response to a request from the government of Angola, sent thousands of volunteer troops to that country to help defeat the invading armed forces of South Africa's apartheid regime. Pretoria was determined to block the Angolan people from realizing their hard-fought independence from Portugal, set for November 11, 1975. The apartheid rulers recognized that the crumbling of the Portuguese empire, the last bastion of European colonialism on the African continent, would provide impetus in South Africa itself to struggles to end white minority rule.

The Cuban government named its internationalist mission in Angola Operation Carlotta, after the slave who led an 1843 rebellion in Cuba's Matanzas Province—the site of the July 26 rally. When the Cuban volunteers arrived, South African troops had already pressed more than four hundred miles into Angolan territory and antigovernment forces had reached the outskirts of the capital city of Luanda. By late March 1976, however, the last invading forces had been pushed back over Angola's southern border into Namibia, at that time still a South African colony.

This initial defeat of apartheid's army gave new impetus to the struggle for a nonracial, democratic republic inside South Africa. In June 1976 young people took to the streets in Soweto and other Black townships across the country. In the years that followed, the surge of protests gave birth to a new network of popular committees and antiapartheid organizations on both the local and national level. Superexploited workers waged strikes and formed trade unions in defiance of government bans.

The new rise of struggles reinforced the African National Congress, which had been banned in 1960 and many of whose leaders, including Mandela, were imprisoned for their antiapartheid activities. The advancing struggle inside the country increased the pariah status and international isolation of the apartheid regime. In limited and uneven ways, imperialist governments in Europe, North America, Asia, and the Pacific acceded to mounting demands by antiapartheid forces to impose economic, sports, cultural, and other sanctions against South Africa.

Over the next twelve years the apartheid rulers repeatedly conducted military operations penetrating deep into Angolan territory. Together with the bipartisan government in Washington, Pretoria armed and financed the forces of UNITA (National Union for the Total Independence of Angola), which carried out counterrevolutionary terrorist operations in southern Angola.

In November 1987, however, in the face of a critical situation in which South African troops had encircled Cuito Cuanavale in southeast Angola, Cuba made the decision to send thousands of volunteer reinforcements and massive amounts of weaponry and supplies. By March 1988 the South African troops had been dealt a decisive military defeat at Cuito Cuanavale by the combined forces of the Cuban volunteers, the Angolan army, and fighters from SWAPO (South West Africa People's Organisation). The South African invaders were forced to withdraw from Angola; in subsequent negotiations the apartheid regime ceded independence to Namibia, which celebrated the end of racist colonial domination and the establishment of its own government in March 1990.

By puncturing once and for all the myth of the white supremacists' invincibility, the outcome at Cuito Cuanavale gave another impulse to the battle against apartheid inside South Africa. The self-assurance of South Africa's capitalist rulers took heavy blows, and tactical divisions among them deepened. On February 2, 1990, the government of Prime Minister F.W. de Klerk announced the unbanning of the African National Congress and several other antiapartheid organizations. Nine days later, on February 11, Nelson Mandela triumphantly walked out of Victor Verster Prison near Cape Town, free for the first time in twenty-seven and a half years.

In his speech to the Matanzas rally, Mandela paid tribute to the unparalleled contribution that Cuba's internationalist volunteers made to the African peoples' struggle for independence, freedom, and social justice. "The crushing defeat of the racist army at Cuito Cuanavale was a victory for the whole of Africa!" Mandela said. "The defeat of the apartheid army was an inspiration to the struggling people inside South Africa! Without the defeat of Cuito Cuanavale our organizations would not have been unbanned! The defeat of the racist army at Cuito Cuanavale has made it possible for me to be here today! . . . Cuito Cuanavale has been a turning point in the struggle to free the continent and our country from the scourge of apartheid!"

Responding to Mandela's tribute, Castro explained that revolutionary Cuba had staked everything—including the existence of the revolution itself—in committing such major military forces to the battle at Cuito Cuanavale. In doing so, said Castro—repeating a theme that has run through many of his speeches in recent years—the Cuban government and people once again showed in practice why internationalism is blood and bone of the revolution, and why any retreat from aiding those fighting for national liberation or socialism elsewhere in the world would be the death knell of the Cuban revolution itself.

As Castro explained in a December 1988 speech to a rally of half a million people in Havana, including many men and women from the Cuban armed forces and Territorial Troop Militia: "Whoever is incapable of fighting for others will never be capable of fighting for himself. And the heroism shown by our forces, by our people in other lands, faraway lands, must also serve to let the imperialists know what awaits them if one day they force us to fight on this land here." (Fidel Castro, *In Defense of Socialism: Four Speeches on the Thirtieth Anniversary of the Cuban Revolution* [New York: Pathfinder, 1989], p. 28.)

The internationalist course charted in Angola is central to the life-or-death questions confronting the Cuban revolution today that are addressed by Castro in the speech printed here. Washington has never forgiven the Cuban people for their declaration of independence from U.S. neocolonialism proclaimed in 1959; it has never forgiven them for the social revolution they began three decades ago. Castro describes some of the lasting social gains and political conquests of that revolution, and he explains why the leadership of the Cuban revolution will continue along the historic line of march charted almost 150 years ago by Karl Marx and Frederick Engels—toward a world where human beings live and work together as brothers and sisters, instead of being forced to prey on each other like wolves.

From the mid-1970s through the mid-1980s, internationalist missions such as those carried out by hundreds of thousands of Cubans in Angola—as well as in Grenada, Nicaragua, and elsewhere—were the main social and political force helping to mobilize and politically inspire working people in Cuba. Internationalist commitment stood counterposed to the political disorientation fostered by the policies, institutions, and priorities that had begun to be systematically implemented in Cuba in the early 1970s, largely copied from the Soviet Union and Eastern European countries. When the leadership of the Communist Party of Cuba in 1986 launched what is known as the rectification process, aimed at combating the social and political roots of this decade-long depoliticization, a major impetus to this effort was the determination to bring the political spirit and confidence generated by the internationalist missions in Angola into the daily battle to advance the revolution at home.

In the final portion of the Matanzas speech, Castro takes up the arguments of those who say that socialism was the loser in the Cold War and that capitalism has emerged the victor. He explains the realities of intensifying interimperialist competition today and catalogs the economic and social devastation capitalism is wreaking on the peoples of Latin America. Capitalism, he notes, is something the Cuban people know well, inside and out, from their own painful history. This historical experience underlies Cuba's refusal to return to the slave barracks of capitalist exploitation and imperialist domination. Cuban revolutionists, Castro emphasizes, are more convinced than ever that the future for humanity is not backward to "private enterprise and the free market," but forward to a world freed of the poverty, racism, and exploitation generated by capitalism.

❖

In closing his remarks to the Matanzas rally, Nelson Mandela told the thousands gathered there what it meant to him to be awarded the José Martí medal by Cuba's Council of State. "It is a source of strength and hope," he said, because "this award is given for the recognition that the people of South Africa stand on their feet and are fighting for their freedom."

This, above all, is the thread that runs through these speeches: the determination of the peoples of South Africa and Cuba to fight for a new and better world. "No matter what the odds, no matter under what difficulties," Mandela said at Matanzas, you have to struggle. "There can be no surrender! It is a case of freedom or death!"

Mary-Alice Waters
September 12, 1991

January 1, 1959 — The Cuban revolution triumphs over the U.S.-backed dictatorship.

March 21, 1960 — South African police open fire on a crowd of Black protesters at Sharpeville, killing sixty-nine. The apartheid regime subsequently proclaims a state of emergency and bans the ANC and other antiapartheid organizations.

August 5, 1962 — Mandela is captured by South African police. He is convicted and sentenced to five years' imprisonment for incitement to strike and leaving the country without a passport.

June 11, 1964 — Mandela, already serving a prison term, and seven ANC leaders are found guilty of sabotage in the Rivonia trial and are sentenced to life imprisonment.

1965 — Cuban revolutionary leader Ernesto Che Guevara aids liberation forces in the Congo.

November 5, 1975 — Cuba decides to send troops to Angola to combat a South African invasion endangering Angola's upcoming independence. By late March 1976 the South African forces are driven back across Angola's border with Namibia.

June 16, 1976 — Police open fire on protesting South African schoolchildren in Soweto, sparking the first sustained nationwide protests since 1960.

November 1987 — South African troops encircle Angolan forces at Cuito Cuanavale, creating a critical situation for the Angolan government. Cuba decides to send thousands of reinforcements and sufficient military equipment to prevent a South African victory.

January-March 1988 — Cuban troops, together with Angolan and SWAPO troops, repulse five South African assaults and break the siege of Cuito Cuanavale.

Immediately afterward, Cuban, Angolan, and SWAPO forces begin to drive the South African troops back toward Angola's southern border.

July 13, 1988 — Representatives of the United States, South Africa, Angola, and Cuba sign a fourteen-point statement setting a framework for South African withdrawal from Angola and Namibia's independence from South African colonial rule. A final agreement is signed December 22.

February 2, 1990 — The South African government announces the unbanning of the ANC and other organizations.

February 11, 1990 — Mandela is released from prison after twenty-seven and a half years.

March 21, 1990 — Namibia celebrates its independence from South African rule.

May 25, 1991 — The last Cuban troops leave Angola under an agreement between the Cuban and Angolan governments.

July 25-27, 1991 — Mandela visits Cuba.

NELSON MANDELA

Mandela speaking at July 26 rally. (Photo: Mary-Alice Waters/*Militant*)

NELSON MANDELA

We will ensure that the poor and rightless will rule the land of their birth

First Secretary of the Communist Party, President of the Council of State and of the government of Cuba, President of the Socialist Republic of Cuba, Commander in Chief, Comrade Fidel Castro;

Cuban internationalists, who have done so much to free our continent;

Cuban people; comrades and friends:

It is a great pleasure and honor to be present here today, especially on so important a day in the revolutionary history of the Cuban people. Today Cuba commemorates the thirty-eighth anniversary of the storming of the Moncada. Without Moncada, the *Granma* expedition, the struggle in the Sierra Maestra, and the extraordinary victory of January 1, 1959, would never have occurred.[1]

Today this is revolutionary Cuba, internationalist Cuba, the country that has done so much for the peoples of Africa.

We have long wanted to visit your country and express the many feelings that we have about the Cuban revolution, about the role of Cuba in Africa, southern Africa, and the world.[2]

The Cuban people hold a special place in the hearts of the people of Africa. The Cuban internationalists have made a contribution to African independence, freedom, and justice, unparalleled for its principled and selfless character.

From its earliest days the Cuban revolution has itself been a source of inspiration to all freedom-loving people.

We admire the sacrifices of the Cuban people in maintaining their independence and sovereignty in the face of a vicious imperialist-orchestrated campaign to destroy the impressive gains made in the Cuban revolution.

We too want to control our own destiny. We are determined that the people of South Africa will make their future and that they will continue to exercise their full democratic rights after liberation from apartheid. We do not want popular participation to cease at the moment when apartheid goes. We want to have the moment of liberation open the way to ever-deepening democracy.

We admire the achievements of the Cuban revolution in the sphere of social welfare. We note the transformation from a country of imposed backwardness to universal literacy. We acknowledge your advances in the fields of health, education, and science.

There are many things we learn from your experience. In particular we are moved by your affirmation of the historical connection to the continent and people of Africa.

Your consistent commitment to the systematic eradication of racism is unparalleled.

But the most important lesson that you have for us is that no matter what the odds, no matter under what difficulties you have had to struggle, there can be no surrender! It is a case of freedom or death!

I know that your country is experiencing many difficulties now, but we have confidence that the resilient people of Cuba will overcome these as they have helped other countries overcome theirs.

We know that the revolutionary spirit of today was started long ago and that its spirit was kindled by many early fighters for Cuban freedom, and indeed for freedom of all suffering under imperialist domination.

We too are also inspired by the life and example of José Martí, who is not only a Cuban and Latin American hero but justly honored by all who struggle to be free.[3]

We also honor the great Che Guevara, whose revolutionary exploits, including on our own continent, were too powerful for any prison censors to hide from us. The life of Che is an inspiration to all human beings who cherish freedom. We will always honor his memory.[4]

We come here with great humility. We come here with great emotion. We come here with a sense of a great debt that is owed to the people of Cuba. What other country can point to a record of greater selflessness than Cuba has displayed in its relations with Africa?

How many countries of the world benefit from Cuban health workers or educationists? How many of these are in Africa?

Where is the country that has sought Cuban help and has had it refused?

How many countries under threat from imperialism or struggling for national liberation have been able to count on Cuban support?

It was in prison when I first heard of the massive assistance that the Cuban internationalist forces provided to the people of Angola, on such a scale that one hesitated to believe, when the Angolans came under combined attack of South African, CIA-financed FNLA, mercenary, UNITA, and Zairean troops in 1975.[5]

We in Africa are used to being victims of countries wanting to carve up our territory or subvert our sovereignty. It is unparalleled in African history to have another people rise to the defense of one of us.

We know also that this was a popular action in Cuba. We are aware that those who fought and died in Angola were only a small proportion of those who volunteered. For the Cuban people internationalism is not merely a word but something that we have seen practiced to the benefit of large sections of humankind.

We know that the Cuban forces were willing to withdraw shortly after repelling the 1975 invasion, but the continued aggression from Pretoria made this impossible.

Your presence and the reinforcement of your forces in the battle of Cuito Cuanavale was of truly historic significance.

The crushing defeat of the racist army at Cuito Cuanavale was a victory for the whole of Africa!

The overwhelming defeat of the racist army at Cuito Cuanavale provided the possibility for Angola to enjoy peace and consolidate its own sovereignty!

The defeat of the racist army allowed the struggling people of Namibia to finally win their independence!

The decisive defeat of the apartheid aggressors broke the myth of the invincibility of the white oppressors!

The defeat of the apartheid army was an inspiration to the struggling people inside South Africa!

Without the defeat of Cuito Cuanavale our organizations would not have been unbanned!

The defeat of the racist army at Cuito Cuanavale has made it possible for me to be here today!

Cuito Cuanavale was a milestone in the history of the struggle for southern African liberation!

Cuito Cuanavale has been a turning point in the struggle to free the continent and our country from the scourge of apartheid!

Apartheid is not something that started yesterday. The origins of white racist domination go back three and a half centuries to the moment when the first white settlers started a process of disruption and later conquest of the Khoi, San, and other African peoples—the original inhabitants of our country.

The process of conquest from the very beginning engendered a series of wars of resistance, which in turn gave rise to our struggle for national liberation. Against heavy odds, African peoples tried to hold on to their lands. But the material base and consequent firepower of the colonial aggressors doomed the divided tribal chiefdoms and kingdoms to ultimate defeat.

This tradition of resistance is one that still lives on as an inspiration to our present struggle. We still honor the names of the great prophet and warrior Makana, who died while trying to escape from Robben Island prison in 1819, Hintsa, Sekhukhune, Dingane, Moshoeshoe, Bambatha, and other heroes of the early resistance to colonial conquest.

It was against the background of this land seizure and conquest that the Union of South Africa was created in 1910. Outwardly South Africa became an independent state, but in reality power was handed over by the British conquerors to whites who had settled in the country. They were able in the new Union of South Africa to formalize racial oppression and economic exploitation of Blacks.

Following the creation of the union, the passing of the Land Act, purporting to legalize the land seizures of the nineteenth century, gave impetus to the process leading to the formation of the African National Congress on January 8, 1912.[6]

I am not going to give you a history of the ANC. Suffice it to say that the last eighty years of our existence has seen the evolution of the ANC from its earliest beginnings aimed at uniting the African peoples, to its becoming the leading force in the struggle of the oppressed masses for an end to racism and the establishment of a nonracial, nonsexist, and democratic state.

Its membership has been transformed from its early days when they were a small group of professionals and chiefs, etc., into a truly mass organization of the people.

Its goals have changed from seeking improvement of the lot of Africans to instead seeking the fundamental transformation of the whole of South Africa into a democratic state for all.

Its methods of achieving its more far-reaching goals have over decades taken on a more mass character, reflecting the increasing involvement of the masses within the ANC and in campaigns led by the ANC.

Sometimes people point to the initial aims of the ANC and its early composition in order to suggest that it was a reformist organization. The truth is that the birth of the ANC carried from the beginning profoundly revolutionary implications. The formation of the ANC was the first step towards creation of a new South African nation. That conception was developed over time, finding clear expression thirty-six years ago in the Freedom Charter's statement that "South Africa belongs to all who live in it, black and white."[7] This was an unambiguous rejection of the racist state that had existed and an affirmation of the only alternative that we find acceptable, one where racism and its structures are finally liquidated.

It is well known that the state's response to our legitimate democratic demands was, among other things, to charge our leadership with treason and, in the beginning of the sixties, to use indiscriminate massacres. That and the banning of our organizations left us with no choice but to do what every self-respecting people, including the Cubans, have done—that is, to take up arms to win our country back from the racists.

I must say that when we wanted to take up arms we approached numerous Western governments for assistance and we were never able to see any but the most junior ministers. When we visited Cuba we were received by the highest officials and were immediately offered whatever we wanted and needed. That was our earliest experience with Cuban internationalism.

Although we took up arms, that was not our preference. It was the apartheid regime that forced us to take up arms. Our preference has always been for a peaceful resolution of the apartheid conflict.

The combined struggles of our people within the country as well as the mounting international struggle against apartheid during the 1980s raised the possibility of a negotiated resolution of the apartheid conflict. The decisive defeat of Cuito Cuanavale altered the balance of forces within the region and substantially reduced the capacity of the Pretoria regime to destabilize its neighbors. This, in combination with our people's struggles within the country, was crucial in bringing Pretoria to realize that it would have to talk.

It was the ANC that initiated the current peace process that we hope will lead to a negotiated transfer of power to the people. We have not initiated this process for goals any different from those when we pursued the armed struggle. Our goals remain achievement of the demands of the Freedom Charter and we will settle for nothing less than that.

No process of negotiations can succeed until the apartheid regime realizes that there will not be peace unless there is freedom and that we are not going to negotiate away our just demands. They must understand that we will reject any constitutional scheme that aims at continuing white privileges.

There is reason to believe that we have not yet succeeded in bringing this home to the government, and we warn them that if they do not listen we will have to use our power to convince them.

That power is the power of the people, and ultimately we know that the masses will not only demand but win full rights in a nonracial, nonsexist, democratic South Africa.

But we are not merely seeking a particular goal. We also propose a particular route for realizing it, and that is a route that involves the people all the way through. We do not want a process where a deal is struck over the heads of the people and their job is merely to applaud.

The government resists this at all costs because the question of how a constitution is made, how negotiations take place, is vitally connected to whether or not a democratic result ensues.

The present government wants to remain in office during the entire process of transition. Our view is that this is unacceptable. This government has definite negotiation goals. It cannot be allowed to use its powers as a government to advance its own cause and that of its allies and to use those same powers to weaken the ANC.

And this is exactly what they are doing. They have unbanned the ANC, but we operate under conditions substantially different from that of other organizations. We do not have the same freedom to organize as does Inkatha and other organizations allied to the apartheid regime.[8] Our members are harassed and even killed. We are often barred from holding meetings and marches.

We believe that the process of transition must be controlled by a government that is not only capable and willing to create and maintain the conditions for free political activity. It must also act with a view to ensuring that the transition is towards creating a genuine democracy and nothing else.

The present government has shown itself to be quite unwilling or unable to create a climate for negotiations. It reneges on agreements to release political prisoners and allow the return of exiles. In recent times it has allowed a situation to be created where a reign of terror and violence is being unleashed against the African communities and the ANC as an organization.

We have had ten thousand people murdered in this violence since 1984 and two thousand this year alone. We have always said that this government that boasts of its professional police force is perfectly capable of ending this violence and prosecuting the perpetrators. Not only are they unwilling, we now have conclusive evidence, published in independent newspapers, of their complicity in this violence.[9]

The violence has been used in a systematic attempt to

advance the power of Inkatha as a potential alliance partner of the National Party.[10] There is now conclusive evidence of funds provided by the government—that is, taxpayers' money—to Inkatha.

All of this indicates the necessity to create an interim government of national unity to oversee the transition. We need a government enjoying the confidence of broad sections of the population to rule over this delicate period, ensuring that counterrevolutionaries are not allowed to upset the process and ensuring that constitution making operates within an atmosphere free of repression, intimidation, and fear.

The constitution itself, we believe, must be made in the most democratic manner possible. To us, that can best be achieved through electing representatives to a constituent assembly with a mandate to draft the constitution. There are organizations that challenge the ANC's claim to be the most representative organization in the country. If that is true, let them prove their support at the ballot box.

To ensure that ordinary people are included in this process we are circulating and discussing our own constitutional proposals and draft bill of rights. We want these to be discussed in all structures of our alliance—that is, the ANC, South African Communist Party, and Congress of South African Trade Unions, and amongst the people in general. That way, when people vote for the ANC to represent them in a constituent assembly, they will know not only what the ANC stands for generally, but what type of constitution we want.

Naturally these constitutional proposals are subject to revision on the basis of our consultations with our membership, the rest of the alliance, and the public generally. We want to create a constitution that enjoys widespread support, loyalty, and respect. That can only be achieved if we really do go to the people.

In order to avoid these just demands, various attempts

have been made to undermine and destabilize the ANC. The violence is the most serious, but there are other more insidious methods. At present there is an obsession in the press, amongst our political opponents, and many Western governments with our alliance with the South African Communist Party.

Newspapers continually carry speculations over the number of Communists on our National Executive and allege that we are being run by the Communist Party.

The ANC is not a communist party but a broad liberation movement, including amongst its members Communists and non-Communists. Anyone who is a loyal member of the ANC, anyone who abides by the discipline and principles of the organization, is entitled to belong to the organization.

Our relationship with the SACP as an organization is one of mutual respect. We unite with the SACP over common goals, but we respect one another's independence and separate identity. There has been no attempt whatsoever on the part of the SACP to subvert the ANC. On the contrary, we derive strength from the alliance.

We have no intention whatsoever of heeding the advice of those who suggest we should break from this alliance. Who is offering this unsolicited advice? In the main it is those who have never given us any assistance whatsoever. None of these advisers have ever made the sacrifices for our struggle that Communists have made. We are strengthened by this alliance. We shall make it even stronger.

We are in a phase of our struggle where victory is in sight. But we have to ensure that this victory is not snatched from us. We have to ensure that the racist regime feels maximum pressure right till the end and that it understands that it must give way, that the road to peace, freedom, and democracy is irresistible.

That is why sanctions must be maintained. This is not the time to reward the apartheid regime. Why should they be rewarded for repealing laws which form what is recognized as an international crime? Apartheid is still in place. The regime must be forced to dismantle it, and only when that process is irreversible can we start to think of lifting the pressure.

We are very concerned at the attitude that the Bush administration has taken on this matter. It was one of the few governments that was in regular touch with us over the question of sanctions, and we made it clear that lifting sanctions was premature. That administration nevertheless, without consulting us, merely informed us that American sanctions were to be lifted. We find that completely unacceptable.

It is in this context that we value our friendship with Cuba very, very much. When you, Comrade Fidel, yesterday said that our cause is your cause, I know that that sentiment came from the bottom of your heart and that that is the feeling of all the people of revolutionary Cuba.

You are with us because both of our organizations, the Communist Party of Cuba and the ANC, are fighting for the oppressed masses, to ensure that those who make the wealth enjoy its fruits. Your great apostle José Martí said: "With the poor people of this earth I want to share my fate."

We in the ANC will always stand with the poor and rightless. Not only do we stand with them. We will ensure sooner rather than later that they rule the land of their birth, that in the words of the Freedom Charter, "the people shall govern." And when that moment arrives, it will have been made possible not only by our efforts but through the solidarity, support, and encouragement of the great Cuban people.

I must close my remarks by referring to an event which you have all witnessed. Comrade Fidel Castro conferred upon me the highest honor this country can award. I am very much humbled by this award, because I do not think I deserve it. It is an award that should be given to those who have already won the freedom of their peoples. But it is a source of strength and hope that this award is given for the recognition that the people of South Africa stand on their feet and are fighting for their freedom.

We sincerely hope that in these days that lie ahead we will prove worthy of the confidence which is expressed in this award.

Long live the Cuban revolution!

Long live Comrade Fidel Castro!

FIDEL CASTRO

Castro speaking at July 26 rally. (Photo: Mary-Alice Waters/*Militant*)

FIDEL CASTRO

We will never return to the slave barracks

Dear Comrade Nelson Mandela; distinguished and illustrious political figures who are here with us this afternoon; relatives of those who died in the revolutionary struggle; guests; comrades of Matanzas and the entire country:

It is truly a great honor for us to have Nelson Mandela here in our country and attending this event. [*Applause*] I'm not sure if we are fully conscious of the symbolism this entails and, above all, of the value of his example in these times—in these shameful times when so many are pulling down their banners, in these indecorous times when so many repent having once been progressive, not to mention socialists or Communists or friends of Communists.

If one wanted an example of an absolutely upright man, that man, that example would be Mandela. [*Applause*] If one wanted an example of an unshakably firm, courageous, heroic, calm, intelligent, and capable man, that example and that man would be Mandela. [*Applause*] I did not just reach this conclusion after having met him in person, after having had the privilege of talking with him, after having had the great honor of receiving him in our country. I have thought this for many years. I identify him as one of the most extraordinary symbols of this era.

That is what I think of him and his people, for if we are

to speak of the most just of causes, it is the cause they have represented. If there is anything odious and repugnant in this world, where there are so many odious and repugnant things, it is apartheid. Who invented it? Communists, socialists, socialism? [*Shouts of "No!"*] No! This invention expresses the essence of capitalism; it was invented by colonialism, neocolonialism, fascism.

In what way is apartheid different from the practice in effect for centuries of dragging tens of millions of Africans from their land and bringing them to this hemisphere to enslave them, to exploit them to the last drop of their sweat and blood? Who would know this better than the people of Matanzas, since here in this part of western Cuba there were perhaps more than 100,000 slaves. In the first half of the last century there were as many as 300,000 slaves in Cuba, and one of the provinces that had the most slaves was this one, which was also the scene of great uprisings. For this reason there is nothing so just nor so legitimate as the monument to the rebellious slave that has just been erected in this province. [*Applause*]

Apartheid is capitalism and imperialism in its fascist form and involves the idea of superior and inferior races.

But the Black people of South Africa not only have had to confront apartheid, they have also had to confront the most brutal inequality and political repression, and they have had to confront the cruelest economic exploitation. They have had to confront these three great tragedies. Because of this I believe there can be no greater cause in our era than the one headed by the ANC, Comrade Mandela, and the many other capable and brilliant leaders of that organization, several of whom we have had the privilege of meeting here in our country.

Today those in the West are trying to ingratiate themselves with Africa, trying to ingratiate themselves with those who hate apartheid. But the fact is that apartheid was created by the West, by the capitalist and imperialist West.

The real truth is that the West supported apartheid; they supplied it with technology, countless billions in investments, and vast quantities of arms; and they also gave it political support. No, imperialism did not break ties with apartheid, it did not blockade apartheid; imperialism maintained and continues to maintain excellent relations with apartheid. It was Cuba that had to be blockaded,[11] Cuba, where the vestiges of apartheid—that is, racial discrimination—disappeared a long time ago. Cuba had to be blockaded as punishment for its revolution, as punishment for its social justice—but never apartheid. They took some halfhearted economic measures against apartheid, which did not have the least significance.

And now, as Mandela himself told me, they are asking why the ANC is a friend of Cuba, why it has relations with Cuba and—as Mandela told me here—why it has relations with the South African Communist Party, as if the specter of communism were still haunting the world. [*Applause*] They are asking why it has relations with this small country that was always so loyal to the cause of the South African people in their struggle against apartheid? This shows the logic of the reactionaries and the imperialists.

It would not be right for us to emphasize Cuba's modest contribution to the cause of those peoples, but on hearing Mandela's speech, comrades, I believe that he paid the greatest and most profound tribute that has ever been paid to our internationalist fighters. [*Applause*] I believe that his words will remain, as if they were written in gold letters, as an homage to our combatants. He was generous, very generous; he recalled the epic feat our people performed in Africa, where all the spirit of this revolution was manifested, all its heroism and steadfastness.

Fifteen years we spent in Angola! Hundreds upon hundreds of thousands of Cubans went there and thousands more went to other countries. That was the epoch in which imperialism would have given anything to see Cuba withdraw from Angola and end its solidarity with the peoples of Africa. But our firmness was greater than all the pressures and was greater than any benefit our country might have gained had we given in to imperialist demands—as if there could ever be any benefit in abandoning principles and betrayal.

We are proud of what we have done, and our troops came back from Angola victorious. But who has said this the way he has? Who has expressed it with such honesty, such eloquence? What we have not said, because basic modesty prevented us, he has expressed here with infinite generosity, recalling that our combatants made it possible for the sister Republic of Angola to maintain its integrity and achieve peace; that our combatants contributed to the existence of an independent Namibia. He added that our combatants contributed to the struggle of the South African people and of the ANC. He said that the battle of Cuito Cuanavale changed the balance of forces and opened up new possibilities.

We were not unaware of the importance of the effort we made there from 1975 up to the last great feat, which was accepting the challenge of Cuito Cuanavale. This was at a distance greater than that between Havana and Moscow, which one can travel in a thirteen-hour nonstop flight. To get from Havana to Luanda is about a fourteen- or fifteen-hour flight, and Cuito Cuanavale was over in the southeastern corner of Angola, more than 1,000 kilometers from Luanda. That was where our country had to accept the challenge.

As Mandela was telling you, in this action the revolution put everything at stake, it put its own existence at stake, it risked a huge battle against one of the strongest powers located in the area of the Third World, against one of the richest powers, with significant industrial and technological development, armed to the teeth, at such a great distance from our small country and with our own resources, our own arms. We even ran the risk of weakening our defenses, and we did so. We used our ships and ours alone, and we used our equipment to change the relationship of forces, which made success possible in that battle. I'm not aware of any other time when a war broke out at such a distance between so small a country and such a great power as that possessed by the South African racists.

We put everything at stake in that action, and it was not the first time. I believe we also put an awful lot at stake in 1975 when we sent our troops to fight the South African invasion of Angola.

I repeat: we were there for fifteen years. Perhaps it should not have taken so long, because the way we saw it, that problem had to be solved; simply put, South Africa had to be prevented from invading Angola. That was our strategic conception: if we wanted peace in Angola, if we wanted security in Angola, we had to prevent South Africa from invading Angola. And if we wanted to prevent the South Africans from invading, we had to assemble the forces and the weapons necessary to prevent them from doing so. We did not have all the equipment to do this, but that was our conception.

The truly critical situation occurred in Cuito Cuanavale, where there were no Cubans at the time because the closest Cuban unit was about two hundred kilometers to the west. This brought us to the decision to employ the troops and the weapons necessary—on our own initiative and at our own risk—and to send whatever was necessary, even if it meant taking it from here.

Cuito Cuanavale is the site that became historic, but the operations extended along a line hundreds of kilometers long, and out of these operations a movement of great strategic importance toward southwest Angola developed. All of this is symbolized by the name Cuito Cuanavale, which is where the crisis began; but about 40,000 Cuban and Angolan soldiers with more than 500 tanks, hundreds of artillery pieces, and about 1,000 antiaircraft weapons—the great majority of these antiaircraft weapons of ours were transferred from here—advanced toward Namibia, supported by our air force and an airstrip constructed in a matter of weeks.

I'm not going to speak here about the strategic and tactical details of the battles, I'll leave that to the historians. But we were determined, together with the Angolans, to put an end to the invasions of Angola once and for all. The events turned out the way we had foreseen—and we don't want to offend or humiliate anybody—because when this new balance of forces developed (and by then we had assembled troops that were invincible and unstoppable), the conditions for negotiations were created, in which we participated for months.

We could have waged big battles there, but given the new situation it was better to resolve the problem of Angola's integrity and Namibia's independence at the negotiating table. We knew—how could we not know!—that those events would have a profound effect on the life of South Africa itself, and this was one of the reasons, one of the motives, one of the great incentives that pushed us on. Because we knew that once the problem in Angola was resolved, the forces that were fighting against apartheid would also benefit from our struggles.

Have we said it this way before? No, never, and perhaps we never would have said this, because, in the first place, we believe that above and beyond whatever international solidarity the ANC has had, above and beyond the enormous support from abroad —of public opinion in some cases, of armed action in our case—the decisive and determining factor behind the ANC's successes was the heroism, the spirit of sacrifice and struggle of the South African people led by the ANC. [*Applause*]

This man, in these times of cowardice and so many things, has come to tell us what he told us this afternoon. It is something that can never be forgotten and it reveals the human, moral, and revolutionary dimension of Nelson Mandela. [*Applause*]

I have not only valued Mandela's words about us and the beautiful homage he paid to our internationalist fighters, demonstrating to us that the bloodshed, the sacrifices, the efforts, and the sweat of so many Cubans were not in vain. I have also greatly appreciated his wise, intelligent, precise words, which reveal true revolutionary tactics and strategy.

He has explained here with impressive clarity what they propose and what they want, how they hope to achieve it and how they are sure they will accomplish it. So we have here this man who spent dozens of years in prison thinking, reflecting, studying, and struggling, and who became an extraordinary political leader, an extraordinary and invincible fighter.

We are sure that now nothing and no one can prevent the success of this noble, humane, and just struggle, which he has summed up as a struggle for an egalitarian, democratic, and nonracial society.

And believe me, comrades, the ANC is confronting a truly complex and difficult task, because despite the fact that it has the support of the great majority of the South African people, the reactionaries have quite a few tricks and stratagems, quite a few maneuvers that they have used to block the South African people's access to its goals. But I think that if there is something that rises above these difficulties, it is the talent of Nelson Mandela and the ANC leaders. [*Applause*]

We feel encouraged on this July 26, and we feel tremendously honored by the presence and the words of such an illustrious political leader and revolutionary. We will never forget them! [*Applause*]

Comrades, in the midst of so many things that are truly moving and of great historical significance, I feel it my duty to talk about other matters that are not so significant, not so historic, but that are also enormously important for us. I must speak a bit—and you won't be able to demand a lot—about this place, this land where, as I was saying before, the slaves used to do the work and where it is now done by free men and women. [*Applause*]

Now it is we who cut the cane. We used to carry it, but now this is done by machines; no one should be alarmed if at some point we have to carry it by hand again, and I wonder if we would carry it or not. [*Applause and shouts of "Yes!"*] Now it is we who pull out all kinds of weeds. Now it is we who cultivate the land, who harvest the fruit. Now it is we who create the wealth. This is the activity of a free people; this is socialism. It is not the activity of the poor, the outcast, the immigrants who replaced the slaves; it is not the unemployed who lined up outside the sugarcane plantations. It is we, all of us, to a greater or lesser extent, because in these times we have also seen engineers, doctors, and scientists participating in the agricultural mobilizations.[12] And because every year we see our students, hundreds of thousands of students participating in the program where the schools go to the countryside and studying at the schools in the countryside, or working in factories, or assembling bicycles, or producing spare parts. We see all of our young people participating in these physical efforts that the slaves and later the outcasts, the poor, the disinherited, the unemployed, or the underemployed used to do. This also has great historical significance.

When one talks about the work that the people of Matanzas have done, one talks about what they have created and are creating with their hands, everywhere. Let us not emphasize now that we're imperfect, which we already know. Let us not emphasize that we have many deficiencies; we know that and we're not going to forget it. Let us emphasize instead the efforts that our people are making today; let us emphasize their virtues, their capacity for sacrifice, the fruits of their efforts.

We should note that in 1990—a difficult year and the

year in which the special period began[13]—and in the first part of 1991, the residents of Matanzas completed 232 construction projects, some of a social and others of an economic nature, primarily economic ones. They range from the small port for supertankers to the highway between Matanzas and Varadero being completed, to dams, minidams, irrigation and sewage systems, rice irrigation systems, a steel foundry, light industry factories, food industry facilities, hog-farming centers, pasturing areas, and an infinite number of projects on which the residents of Matanzas have been working with special fervor in the last few months—because we should also include the special efforts they have made for the July 26 celebration—but it added up to 232 projects. There are also polyclinics, new hospital wings, and day-care centers—programs that were in progress and that are now completed.

We cannot forget that the most important petroleum deposits in the country are found in Matanzas and that Matanzas produces about half a million tons of petroleum. This is heavy petroleum with quite a bit of sulfur, but it solves a lot of problems. Various factories run on this petroleum, cement factories run on this petroleum, various products are being made from derivatives of this petroleum. I asked the director of this enterprise here what had been the level of production in 1990 and this year, and he said, "About half a million." I asked him, "Couldn't more be produced?" "Yes," he said, "we could have produced 600,000 this year, but we haven't had the ships to transport this petroleum." I asked him how the wells were going, and the causeways, how the work was going despite the difficulties. The work is moving along; already some oil wells constructed on the causeways are functioning; because Matanzas Province is the country's number one petroleum producer.

Matanzas Province produces more than 40 percent of the country's citrus fruits. [*Shouts of "Jagüey!"*] Jagüey, yes, Jagüey, more than 40 percent of the country's citrus fruits! [*Applause*] And this production level has risen something like thirty or forty times, and nowadays it's about 46,000 tons. This is one of the largest educational-production complexes that exists anywhere, with over sixty schools.

Matanzas Province has the most important tourist resort in the country, Varadero—although it's not the only one. [*Applause*]

Matanzas Province earns $77 million in gross income—I say gross because we have to deduct some expenses in dollars—$77 million in 1990! And they hope to reach $100 million in gross income in 1991, so you can appreciate the rate at which this program is advancing. Some day Matanzas Province could earn hundreds of millions of dollars, when this program is finished—hundreds of millions of dollars every year, when we have the tens of thousands of hotel rooms that we should have there.

The Varadero construction contingent, which also was awarded its certificate here, has built projects worth 50 million pesos in half a year—half a year![14] And they hope to reach a total of 100 million pesos' worth of construction this year. [*Applause*] An extremely powerful construction work force of 7,000 people has been developed here.

So that you have an idea, this construction contingent in Matanzas, in Varadero alone, will have constructed in one year buildings comparable in value to those for the Pan American Games,[15] which have been built in thirty-three months. This is truly a great effort! [*Applause*]

Yesterday we inaugurated the Pan American facilities; there were over twenty new facilities and over forty remodeled facilities. Thousands of full-time workers and hundreds of thousands of volunteers participated in these projects, which were worth about the same as what the contingent built in Varadero this year.

Matanzas is one of Cuba's great sugar producers. During the years of the revolution, Matanzas produced more than a million tons in three different years, and is working on making this the ordinary figure.

In honor of Matanzas, we should mention that one of the new sugar mills built by the revolution, the most recent one, named after Mario Muñoz, has become the most efficient of all the new sugar mills built by the revolution.[16] [*Applause*]

I talked with the comrades from one enterprise or another about these things when they came up here to receive their certificates. None of the other new sugar mills has produced as much as 118,000 tons. This also shows how the revolution has advanced, how it is capable of building a sugar mill with such a great capacity, with over 60 percent of the components made in Cuba. [*Applause*] Look how far we slaves have come! How far we slaves have come! [*Applause*]

In Matanzas we have university branches—one of the directors came here—that teach different specialities in mechanics, economics, etc. In Matanzas 1,300 students have graduated from the local medical school and thousands have graduated from the teacher-training institutes.

How far we slaves have come!

Matanzas has complete educational facilities, from the Karl Marx School—whose name we don't plan to change—to many schools of varying types. [*Applause*] There's another school in Havana, a very important one, the Vladimir Ilyich Lenin School—whose name we also don't plan to change. [*Applause*] And there is another one—I think it's in Pinar del Río, yes, it's a very good one—called the Frederick Engels School—and of course we're not planning to change that name either. [*Applause*] Just as we're not planning to change the name of the José Martí School in Holguín, [*Applause*] or the Máximo Gómez School in Camagüey, or the Antonio Maceo School in Santiago de Cuba, [*Shouts of "The Che Guevara School!"*] or the Che Guevara School—you took the words right out of my mouth—in Santa Clara. [*Applause*] Because a revolution like ours does not change its ideas or its names. [*Applause*]

How far we slaves have come!

I repeat that Matanzas has a complete educational system. There are numerous schools of all kinds. I'm not going to enumerate them—a university, primary schools, teaching hospitals, cultural institutions—about two hundred, very appropriate for the Athens of Cuba, as Matanzas was rightly called in other times and should still be called, since it symbolizes the educational level this province has achieved. [*Applause*] Its sports institutions—someone over there has the total number of medals that Matanzas residents have won during these years of the revolution. As Guillén would have put it, "Matanzas has what it had to have!"[17] [*Applause*]

But above all, we have our dignity and our independence, our bravery and our heroism, even in the difficult times in which we live—and we will have them even if times become yet more difficult.

What are they going to tell us about? About the past? About capitalism? [*Shouts of "No!"*] About private property? About large landed estates? About corporations? [*Shouts of "No!"*] About imperialism? About neocolonialism? Do we want to hear about all that garbage? [*Shouts of "No!"*] What else can I call all that?

So what are they going to tell us about? About the days when there were beggars? What are they going to tell us about? About the days of prostitution? [*Shouts of "No!"*] About the systematic plunder of the public treasury? About cheap politicking? About the merciless exploitation of the workers? About landless peasants, or peasants paying rent, a percentage of what they produced?

What are they going to tell us about? About that society of racial discrimination? Where in some provincial capitals whites walked on one side and Blacks on the other, on different streets, or on different paths in the park. I don't remember whether it was in Santa Clara or Villa Clara where these things went on; I can imagine the exclusive spots here. It took different forms.

What are they going to tell us about? About discrimination? About prostitution and all the vices of that society? About barefoot children begging and not attending school? About illiteracy? About women working as domestic servants and in open or de facto prostitution? [*Shouts of "No!"*] They better not come to us with stories about their capitalism, their market economies, and all that madness, because we already know about that, and I think we remember it quite well.

What are they going to tell me about Birán, where I grew up as the son of a landowner, where I was able to see the results of capitalism in hundreds and hundreds of children there who never got past first, second, or third grade—if they went to school at all. And if someone reached sixth grade he was considered really sharp and they made him a foreman or something like that.

I have nothing bad to say about my father as a man, since I always remember his generosity, although his social position was no longer that of the son of a humble peasant from Galicia, but rather a man who owned large plots of land.

I learned about capitalism without having suffered from it, through observation. Later I had a lot of time to think and ponder about that society of the whip and of the Rural Guard, the Rural Guard that the U.S. forces organized here when they disarmed the *mambí* army.[18] But this time they were unable to disarm the Rebel Army, and the whip and the Rural Guard were done away with. [*Applause*]

What are they going to tell us about? [*Shouts of "Fidel, Fidel" and "For sure, Fidel, give the Yankees hell!"*] What are they going to convince us of? What are they going to tell the residents of Matanzas about? [*Shouts of "We have a strong socialism!"*] And what are they going to tell the women of Matanzas about? [*Shouts of "Nothing!" and "Whatever is necessary, Fidel, whatever is necessary!"*]

Before the revolution women made up only 10 percent of the work force and now they are 40 percent. And not only that. But those women facing discrimination, without any future other than the one I mentioned, that of domestic work, of open or de facto prostitution—because sometimes they chose her for a particular job to serve as a lure or an attraction for shoppers—those women now constitute about 60 percent of the technical work force of Matanzas. [*Applause*] Thus, the bulk of the trained minds in this province are women.

How far we slaves have come! [*Applause*]

Who wants to return to the days of the slave barracks? [*Shouts of "No one!"*] And how will they force us to return there? With the threat of hunger perhaps, with a tighter blockade, with imperialist triumphalism following the disasters that have occurred in Eastern Europe? [*Shouts of "No!"*] What can they threaten us with, we the descendants of Maceo and Martí, of Máximo Gómez and Agramonte, of Che and Camilo, of Abel Santamaría and Frank País?[19] [*Prolonged applause*] With the threat of famine, blockades, wars? [*Shouts of "No!"*] We can never experience a tighter blockade and more suffering than what our ancestors suffered, because today we are owners of the land; now it belongs only to the people. Today we are owners of the factories; now they belong only to the people. The people own the means of production and everything else. And we will solve our problems, we will solve them however we must. But we will never return to the slave barracks! [*Shouts and applause*]

They may threaten us with their sophisticated weapons. Perhaps they don't believe they are dealing with a courageous and intelligent people that knows how to fight. And if we fought fourteen thousand kilometers away—however far it was—if we got into the trap at Cuito Cuanavale that the enemies had created and that turned into a trap for them, then here, on our coasts, in our countryside, in our mountains, in our cities, in our canefields, in our ricefields, in our swamps, we will fight as we fought at Cuito Cuanavale. [*Applause*] We will fight even harder than we fought at Cuito Cuanavale, and we will resist for more years than we resisted in Angola, until victory. [*Prolonged applause*]

This is what we can say about the sophisticated weapons of imperialism. And if we weren't among decent people, we could tell them what they should do with their weapons. [*Laughter and applause*]

Our army has millions of men and women ranging from teenagers to the elderly. [*Applause and shouts of "For sure, Fidel, give the Yankees hell!"*]

What are they going to frighten us with, their so-called smart weapons? We are smarter than those weapons and smarter than those who own them. And our weapons can't be underestimated either, above all because behind every one of them is a patriot and a revolutionary. [*Applause*]

We can't say "a pair of pants," like they just shouted over there, [*Laughter*] because that is male chauvinism; there can be pants or skirts, shorts or bathing suits, whatever they want. [*Laughter*] Behind each weapon there will be the type of patriot who can't be fooled, confused, or frightened. So, gentlemen imperialists, with us things are different, with us it's a horse of a different color. We will never go back to the past! [*Applause*]

Ideological battles have to be waged, great ideological battles, because it seems that imperialism may have no enemy in this world now other than little Cuba, this green Caribbean alligator, as Che once called it. [*Applause*]

Already all of its propaganda and resources are no longer directed against the old socialist camp, the USSR, or anyone else, and they are making demands on everybody about Cuba. It is shameful to see how they speak to the USSR, telling it that if it wants any economic aid it has to stop all cooperation with Cuba in all spheres. But that's not all. Recently in a Senate resolution an amendment was introduced about economic relations with China, which stated that China would no longer receive most-favored-nation status—that is a status used in international trade, which the Chinese have and which must be renewed—if China cooperated with Cuba. They address themselves to great powers like the USSR, taking advantage of the current conjuncture to set conditions—conditions! Look at the level of hatred, the thirst for revenge, the desire for vengeance against the revolution, the political and human wretchedness. Of course, I must also say that the Soviets and the Chinese have stated they would not accept any conditions of this sort. [*Applause*] But the pressure is great, very great, and they are threatening not to give any kind of aid.

I really don't know if they can, because one cannot assume that the imperialists are swimming in gold, much less the U.S. imperialists. The capitalists have money, but not enough money to satisfy the demand. At times their positions are humiliating, and it's hard to conceive how they are capable of ordering great countries about with the language they employ, because it shows a lack of respect, of basic respect for the dignity of these governments and the dignity of these peoples. But since some of them are going through difficult situations, they are practically obliged to be heroic in the face of U.S. pressure. It is unheard-of impudence. It would seem that the only place remaining in the world at which to direct their guns is Cuba.

Well, *guns* rhymes with what someone over there said, but I shouldn't repeat it. [*Laughter*] Anyway, *guns* rhymes with a lot of other things. [*Laughter*]

I certainly didn't mean it that way, but I see you're all laughing and I realize it's true, guns [*cañones*] and hearts [*corazones*] rhyme perfectly, [*Laughter*] who can deny it?

[*Applause*] They point their guns at us, all of their guns; that's the truth. Look at how they have honored us, look at the privilege they have granted us of defending the most just ideas in human history, of defending the ideas of socialism and the ideas of Marxism-Leninism. [*Applause*]

No group of apostles came here to teach us Marxism-Leninism. We learned it here, following universal currents, socialist thought, and the thinking of the great revolutionaries of the last century and the present one. Because the more we know imperialism and its miseries the more socialist we feel, the more communist we feel. [*Applause*]

We have just returned from a historic meeting. It was truly historic because for the first time there was a meeting of Latin American leaders—in this case it included two European countries, two Iberian countries—and for the first time we met without Washington giving us the signal.[20] Previously in order for Latin American leaders to meet it was not even necessary to say a word; all the president of the United States had to do was snap his fingers and everyone would run there.

This time it was the Latin Americans who organized the meeting, the Mexicans, and they were courageous enough to invite Cuba—because you have to be courageous to invite Cuba—and the Mexicans were courageous, which the United States did not like at all. [*Applause*] And when they could not keep us from going, they devoted themselves to trying to sabotage the trip in a variety of ways, making all sorts of plans—as one might assume—to create problems and difficulties. But it seems all their attempts backfired.

They mounted an enormous propaganda effort. Nevertheless, among the masses there—and not only among the masses, among famous people, political leaders in the country, everybody—and in a very special way among the people and among the people of Guadalajara, the expressions of solidarity and affection toward Cuba were extraordinary, truly extraordinary! [*Applause*] This shows that the peoples do not forget history, that imperialist crimes are not forgotten, that the enormous propaganda campaign against the revolution does not go over well with those who have a class instinct and realize who it is that stands with the world's poor, as Mandela put it, evoking Martí. They know who stands with the oppressed and the exploited and they know who stands against the exploiters, the conquerors, the colonizers, the neocolonizers, and the plunderers. They know! So we felt like family there as we do here.

We had to walk a kilometer. There were tens of thousands of people. I lagged behind because journalists and many people stopped me. I couldn't go in front, I was practically the last. I was there alone, like a dove; [*Laughter*] but I was completely happy. The more plans they had prepared the happier I was and the more I liked it. [*Applause*] I must say in all justice, however, that the Mexican authorities organized the event very well and took the measures they considered necessary, within what was possible, because as you know, certain security measures can be taken only within the framework of what is possible.

The rest is pleasure, because when one scorns the enemy one feels a certain pleasure. I don't believe this to be a defect; it is something I have to thank the enemies for: the pleasure they give me when they go crazy and start inventing things and fail. [*Laughter*]

I said that this was a historic meeting. In addition, I must say that in that gathering of leaders I saw many capable individuals, some of them with outstanding abilities. The United States did everything possible to try to encourage attacks against Cuba by members of that group, to encourage polemics against Cuba. The truth is that they had extremely little success in this regard. We can say that they had very, very little success, really none at all, apart from political and ideological differences, and apart from the fact that a very few of these leaders think in perfect harmony with Washington. I don't mean Washington who founded the United States, I'm talking about the empire's capital.

In general, over and above the ideological differences, an atmosphere of amiability, cordiality, and mutual respect prevailed there. This was true even though I was aware of the moment we're living in, and one of the distinctive features of this moment is the enormous wave of neoliberalism throughout Latin America and throughout the world. We could say that it is practically worldwide, but it is especially strong in Latin America. That is, capitalism is congratulating itself over the political disasters in the Eastern European socialist countries, which have occurred for reasons that are not appropriate for analysis here.

We have our own thoughts about all these issues and we have had our own ideas for a very long time. And among those whose ideas have been exceedingly lucid, clearer than the waters at Varadero, was Che, [*Applause*] like a prophet who could predict the outcome of some of the practices employed in the construction of socialism. This is apart from historical factors and the fact that these societies were begun in the poorest countries of Europe with the aid of a country like the USSR, which had been destroyed twice in less than twenty-five years, confronting an empire that at the end of World War II had accumulated all the world's gold and had not lost a single screw in its factories or a single atom of its economic structure during the war years.

A serious and profound study must be made. This is not the right time to do so; everyone must be responsible for their own deeds and their own actions. And the Cuban revolution is historically responsible for its own deeds and its own actions. Note well that I said "its own," because they were our deeds and actions, not those of others. We have our own ideas, our own concepts, and we have done things our own way.

For example, today we do not have to invent small farmers, because we have seventy thousand small farmers, seventy thousand schools for learning about small farmers and how to work and coordinate with them.[21] We do not have to start splitting up state enterprises or things like that, because in our country that would be the insanity of the century. Mazorra mental hospital, with all its capacity, would not be big enough to house the crazy person who would want to do such a thing. I call it Mazorra, the old name of the Havana Psychiatric Hospital, the country's largest and one of the world's best and most famous. So we did things our way.

Here there was no forced collectivization or anything similar to it. There were none of the phenomena that occurred in other places, and if there were some negative things it was because we incorrectly copied others, because the worst thing one can do is copy. This does not mean that we underrate the experience of others in any way; that is different. In addition, no one ever gave us orders and no one ever dared try to give us orders. There has not been, there is not, and there will never be anyone in the world that can give us orders. [*Applause*]

With regard to these problems of socialism: Socialism is very new, just out of the shell. The foundations and the essence of capitalism are thousands of years old—private property, for example. For thousands of years not only have things been objects of private property, but people as well, since the time of ancient Greece. In this regard Athens is not very symbolic, except as a historical experience or as just admiration for the art they were able to develop. But it was a slave society, where a handful of people got together in a plaza and said, "This is democracy," and the rest of the citizens had no rights and the immense majority were slaves. If you read the writings of the Greek philosophers, some of them left wills that talk about what they bequeathed; when they drew up a document saying who they would leave their property to, they always said: "I enjoy good health, but in the event of. . . ." In general, that is how all the wills began, and they would go on to state, "I bequeath such-and-such slave to so-and-so." Even the philosophers, who were wise men and believed themselves to be just people, had lots of slaves. That is why we cannot present that type of democracy as an example.

Capitalism comes from Homer's time and even before Homer; its foundations are thousands of years old. Socialism is barely a few decades old, it's in diapers; we can say that socialism is in the stage that maternity hospitals call perinatal. Socialism is in the perinatal phase, that is, the first six or seven days of the baby's life, which are the most dangerous and require special care. We have set up perinatal intensive-care units as part of our program to protect children's health.

In other words, it is logical that socialism, the most just of all ideas, has to pass through various periods and difficulties. In some countries it has disappeared. There are cases like that of the former German Democratic Republic, where hair-raising stories are now coming out. Apartheid in the GDR! Perhaps the ANC will have to give political advice to the Blacks, Asians, mestizos, and others who for one reason or another wound up in the GDR. They are now pursued in the streets and there have been cases in which Vietnamese, Mozambicans, and Angolans have been lynched—I don't know if some Cuban who stayed there has met this fate. Fascist groups persecute them as an expression of xenophobia and racial hatred. This is what has come to replace that society, the rebirth of the most repugnant sentiments of racial hatred, arrogance, and the idea of fascist racial superiority. This news comes independently of other news, because they have begun to be acquainted with the kiss of the devil, the kiss of capitalism, in spite of the fact that they still do not have full-blown capitalism; they are only moving toward capitalism and these sorts of situations are occurring.

There are some who forget that China is a socialist country that firmly maintains the principles of socialism and has 1.1 billion inhabitants—as if this were nothing in a country that has put an end to famine and the calamities that battered that nation for thousands of years. They are now suffering some major disasters, such as floods and rains unseen in a hundred years. But there is the socialist state, the party, and the government, and none of those people will be left abandoned. It is painful, because we know the enormous effort they have made constructing dams and canals, and we know the harm these rains can have for agriculture. But no one will die of hunger there, of that I am sure; and nobody will die for lack of medical attention.

The USSR is experiencing very serious problems; it is impossible to predict how things will evolve. We hope they evolve in the most positive form possible.

All these events have led to an enormous triumphalism on the part of imperialism, and to skepticism among many progressive forces and a large part of the world's left-wing forces. There are people who would rather die of opportunism before remembering that they were once members of a communist party, who are afraid of having belonged to a communist party, who are afraid of the immense honor of having belonged to a communist party. Because being a member of a communist party—regardless of the errors that party may have committed—will always be the greatest honor. Belonging to a party of the poor is not the same as joining the parties and clubs of the millionaires and the plunderers. [*Applause*]

Whatever error Communists can be accused of, they cannot be accused of the exploitation of man by man, or of having supported the exploitation of man by man.

All the things that have occurred have created confusion and a wave of neoliberalism. Other factors have been added to this: the foreign debt and the demands of the International Monetary Fund, the World Bank, and the international financial institutions, which state: "If you don't do this, we won't give you a cent," and they are forced to agree.

There are some who believe in neoliberalism, and there are others who have no other choice than to believe in it, because if they don't they will not get one cent. So there is a wave of privatization. What is in fashion is privatization, private enterprise, and market economies. This is a strange new way of terming things; it cannot be easily understood, and you don't know if those who mention them and repeat them understand what they mean. But market economy, private enterprise, and private property actually have only one name: capitalism, and nothing else. The ideas of socialism are being cast aside as something prehistoric—as if capitalism, colonialism, and neocolonialism were not the truly prehistoric systems, and socialism the genuinely new one.

Some people have said in relation to Cuba: "We want changes." As if we had not made more changes than anyone else in the last thirty years, as if in thirty years we have not made changes that others have not made in three thousand years. And I have told them: What you want is not for us to change, but for us to change back; and that we will never do! This is the reality. [*Applause*]

Of course, what many Latin American leaders have had on their minds more than anything is capitalism and neoliberalism, some more than others, in a situation without alternatives.

There is a new language, a lot of talk about social justice and the redistribution of wealth. At a certain moment I asked for the floor to say that when I heard this stated and repeated, I began to have hallucinations: for a few moments I felt like I was at a meeting of leaders of radical left-wing political parties. I added that this was surely the influence of Orozco's paintings that were on the ceiling of the room where we were meeting, some very revolutionary paintings that were there, but with the imagination of a great painter like Orozco. I said that at any rate I was happy that there was talk of social justice and redistribution of wealth, which perhaps meant that they were gaining awareness. Those were my words, more or less.

There is no doubt that all the political leaders are talking about social justice and the redistribution of wealth; that is not lacking. But I asked myself: Where did injustice come from? Where did inequality come from? Where did poverty come from? Where did underdevelopment come from? Where did all these calamities come from, if not from capitalism? Where did colonialism come from, if not from capitalism? Where did neocolonialism and imperialism come from, if not from capitalism? It would seem that the creators of heaven and earth are to be blamed for the existence of poor people and that the social system has nothing to do with it, that capitalism has nothing to do with it. It's incredible! This is the language, this is the mentality, this is the doctrine.

To want to resolve these problems through capitalism, in a world that has been divided between extremely rich capitalist countries and the majority of extremely poor countries—precisely as a consequence of capitalism, colonialism, neocolonialism, and imperialism—is an incredible illusion. To think that neoliberal formulas are going to promote the miracle of economic development in our countries is an incredible illusion. It's like trying to put out a fire with gasoline.

It's as if we did not know the statistics. There are countries in Latin American where 5 percent of the population receives up to 50 percent of the income, and where 30 or 40 percent of the population receives 10 percent—an incredible level of inequality and injustice.

All this poverty from which the Latin American countries suffer is the direct result of capitalism. But more and more theories are coming out about how private enterprise generates wealth and how in order to have social justice you have to have capitalism, private enterprise, the market economy, and the pure capitalist system, as pure as in the last century. And they try to conceal all the consequences of this under the phrase "redistribution of wealth."

They are redistributing a little bit of wealth over there in Europe and in the countries that looted the world. Although these countries have tens of millions of unemployed, they have something to give to the unemployed for a time. But there are many Latin American countries in which the difference in income between one part of the population and the other is forty to one. Capitalism lacks the capacity, the morals, the ethics, and the will to resolve the problems of poverty.

Well now, how many poor people are there in Latin America? According to a conference held just a few months ago in Quito, Ecuador—a conference on poverty—there are 270 million poor in Latin America. Of these, 84 million are destitute. That is the situation in Latin America as a whole. When I speak of Latin America, I speak of it as a whole, although there are important differences between one country and another. There are countries in Latin America that have extraordinary earnings; because their exports are highly valued on the world market they are very rich, while other countries are much poorer. Those with high earnings have a better situation than those with low earnings. Those with large export earnings are less dependent on international financial institutions and have a bit more room to maneuver.

But the social calamity is everywhere. There are no less than 20 million homeless children in Latin America; some estimate that there are 30 million homeless children in Latin America's streets. There are millions of school-age children who work more than eight hours a day.

The number of children throughout Latin America that

finish elementary school is 44 for every 100 who enroll. This reminds me of Birán; what is happening now in Latin America used to happen there. There was a little public school, one teacher, no resources, nothing. The parents used to take their children to work in the fields or to do some other thing, or else they did not have clothing or shoes or food to go to school. That is, according to the information that I've read, 56 out of every 100 do not make it to sixth grade. You can calculate the percentage that make it to high school. Despite this, millions make it to high school, and then they saturate the universities and afterwards find themselves unemployed. A small fraction of children get to elementary and secondary schools, and despite this there are millions in the universities. This is an explosive force, all these university-educated intellectuals who find themselves unemployed.

The infant mortality rate in Latin America is about 60 per 1,000 live births in the first year of life. The mortality rate for children in the first five years of life—which of course includes those under the age of one—is between 70 and 80 per 1,000. There are countries that have substantially less and there are some that have quite a bit more.

From 30 to 40 percent of the work force is unemployed or underemployed in Latin America. Malnutrition affects 80 to 100 million people. Life expectancy is less than 70 years on the average, much lower than in the developed countries.

Our program of having special schools available to the entire population is something they cannot even dream of. Our family doctor program would seem like a story told by a traveler from a far-off star. The number of teachers or doctors that we have per capita—they cannot even dream about such things. Instead they have doctors sometimes doing other work that has nothing to do with their profession, such as manual labor.

Matanzas itself is an example of what used to happen. In the past there were about 230 doctors here—I believe it was 236—and today there are 1,900; there were 116 nurses and today there are 4,000, including nurses and nurses' aides. Added to this are thousands of technicians, which the health care system did not have in the past.

All these calamities are found in Latin America. All the Latin American capitals are surrounded by slums full of destitute people, and often the number of people who live in shantytowns and favelas in the capital cities is greater than the number who live in normal conditions. All the Latin American capitals are surrounded by slums, without a single exception.

Who is responsible for this? Is capitalism removed from this problem? Are colonialism and neocolonialism removed from it? Is U.S. imperialism removed from this problem? How can they come along now with the formula that what is needed is more capitalism to develop these countries?

We are a country that has depended primarily on sugarcane, we do not have a lot of resources that can be sold throughout the world at any price; we do not have seas of petroleum in our subsoil that give us billions of dollars in income every year. Moreover, our population has nearly as many inhabitants per square kilometer as China does, almost 100 inhabitants per square kilometer. We have to make our living the hard way in our country. Despite this, we export calories for 40 million people in the world. We are now entering into other fields, we are entering into the fields of science, biotechnology, and many other things. We are entering into the field of developing the fabulous natural resources that we have, the beauty of our country and its beaches, which for us has become our petroleum, and we have to make use of them.

There are other fields that we are developing considerably, with the aid of science and technology. We will have to win our place in the world and our economic independence through intelligence and tenacity; in difficult conditions we have no other choice. With the catastrophe in

Eastern Europe, with the USSR going through enormous difficulties, with imperialism more triumphalist than ever, with neoliberalism in fashion, with the imperialists imposing an ever more rigid blockade on us—under these conditions we have to make our own way. This is our most sacred and most basic duty if we want to have a nation, if we want to protect not just the conquests of our revolution but also the sovereignty and independence of this country, which we have worked so hard to achieve.

We are a country with scant resources, yet none of these phenomena that I mentioned exist in Cuba. In Cuba the infant mortality rate last year was 10.7 per 1,000 live births, which is better than the rate in many developed countries; last year's mortality rate for children under five was 14. These are impressive statistics. Our life expectancy is about 76 years of age and rising.

Illiteracy disappeared some time ago. Nearly 100 percent of the children who enter elementary school finish; more than 90 percent of those of age are in secondary school. Workers in some provinces, like Matanzas, average a tenth-grade education.

We do not have slums, as a rule, except for very isolated cases that arise despite our efforts. The phenomenon of malnutrition is insignificant here; undernourished children show up in hospitals due to some illness, or because of family neglect.

It cannot be said that there are no jobs for those who want to work in this country, even during the special period, because there are always a lot of things to be done, even when we lack raw materials in the factories.

Even during the special period, more than twenty thousand university graduates have been given jobs: engineers, economists, agronomists, and others. Just in the area of engineering and economics there are about eight thousand graduates, and we already know where every one of them will go to work. It is very possible that they are not needed now in our factories, but we are not leaving them out in the street; we are putting them alongside another engineer so they keep learning, acquiring experience, so that we have a reserve of engineers and technicians. Our society, which is based on human solidarity, will not put anyone out on the street, it will not leave a single graduate unemployed. We distribute what we have and that is socialism, that is social justice, distributing what we have. [*Applause*] If we have a lot we can distribute a lot, and if we have little we distribute a little, but we distribute what we have, we do not abandon anyone.

There is not a single abandoned mother in this country, either because she is a single mother or has had one or two children—and some have even had up to seven children, which shows a great lack of responsibility. But the state does not let those seven children go hungry; they are all given social security and are cared for.

All workers are protected by social security. The whole population has the right to free health care—even if they need a heart transplant—and the right to education. That is socialism.

Of course, we have declared ourselves enemies of the big monopolies and enemies of the empire, and they will not forgive us for that. How can they forgive the fact that a small country that throughout history they thought they had in their hands, like a ripe apple that falls from the tree, has made a social revolution? They will do everything possible to erase from history this revolutionary process, this example. They will not resign themselves to it.

But that makes two of us who are not going to resign ourselves. They are not going to resign themselves to the revolution and we are never going to resign ourselves to returning to the past. We will never resign ourselves to becoming a neocolony again or a U.S. possession, never! [*Applause*] We will see which of these two is the most tenacious and which of the two is stronger. [*Shouts of "We are!"*]

Latin America is in a dilemma. The problem of Latin America and the Caribbean is not an easy one. There are 446 million inhabitants and within twenty-five years this figure will be 800 million—equal to the current population of India—with all those problems that I spoke about. And there are outstanding political leaders in these countries' governments and other public figures I have met who understand these problems.

Latin America has no alternative but to integrate, to unite. That is what the founders of these republics always dreamed of, that was Bolívar's essential dream,[22] and almost a hundred years later, that of Martí.

That was logical, and for this reason I did not mince words at the meeting. Thinking of the history of this hemisphere since the struggles for independence, I stated: "We could have been everything, yet we are nothing." I was referring to the comparison between the divided, Balkanized Latin America of today in the face of a very powerful and increasingly protectionist European Economic Community; in the face of a power like Japan, which is also very powerful economically and increasingly protectionist; and the United States, the third great economic power among the rich developed countries that control all the world's gold and foreign exchange and run the international credit institutions.

In the face of this new international situation, the number one concern of the United States more and more is its competition with Europe, Japan, and its other partners. It therefore wants to ensure that Latin America remains its backyard, and this is why it launched the so-called Initiative for the Americas. This initiative clashes with the vital and indispensable integration of Latin America because it is based on a series of bilateral accords with the purpose of developing neocolonial trade relations characterized, fundamentally, by unequal terms of trade. They are looking for cheap labor and raw materials for their capital.

The development of this kind of policy clashes with the idea of trade among the Latin American nations and Latin America's economic integration, which is its only possible salvation. Trade among the Latin American countries is insignificant: in 1970 it accounted for 12 percent of exports; now it is 13 percent. In contrast, trade among the great economic powers and the great economic blocs is growing constantly.

This initiative threatens Latin America's integration and threatens to integrate Latin America into the economy of the United States, which is the worst off of the three blocs. No one should imagine that the United States is a bed of roses from the economic point of view. It has become a country incapable of competing; it cannot compete with Europe and it cannot compete with Japan. Within Europe, one of the powers defeated in World War II—Germany—is the most powerful country. Japan, another defeated country, is very powerful.

A U.S. television journalist who interviewed me—he said he wanted to ask me about sports but he spoke very little about sports and the rest was about politics—was telling me that the USSR had been ruined by the arms race with the United States. I told him, it's not just the USSR. The USSR may be the first to be ruined, but you will be the second, because you are also in ruins. Don't sing victory songs, I told him. [*Applause*]

Now, what is happening in the United States? Allow me to continue a bit with this idea so as to make it clear. The United States used to be the center of capitalism, the richest, the most competitive of all countries. Following World War II it enjoyed complete hegemony. And now it has lost these positions. In many important industries such as automobiles, chemicals, electronics, steel, and others it has lost the position it once had, which has been taken up by competitors.

In the years following the war, the rate of return on invested capital was as high as 24 percent. For capitalism, the rate of return on investment is very important, because this is the money available to continue investing and developing. In the 1950s the rate of return was 24 percent, and now it is about a third of that, about 8 percent.

Another very important matter for capitalism, the economists say, is the savings rate: how much of the money people receive that is put into savings. They deposit it in banks, the banks lend it, and this money is invested. The United States has been characterized historically by a high savings rate, for various reasons. A leader who I was conversing with told me that there are some European countries where people save 30 cents out of every dollar they earn, and in the United States people save 5 cents out of every dollar. This is a terrible index for a capitalist country like the United States.

The U.S. debt is $10 trillion—imagine, not 100 billion, or 500 billion, or 1 trillion, but $10 trillion. This includes both the public and private debts—the state owes about $3 trillion, and the rest is owed by businesses and individuals. In other words, that country has a debt twice the size of its Gross National Product; it produces goods and services worth $5 trillion and its debt is $10 trillion. This is a very negative index for that country, and the debt continues to grow.

People have gotten used to living off profits and interest and speculation, and that country spends much more than it produces. Suffice it to say, for example, that now, with a recession that began in the middle of 1990, it was announced that the U.S. budget deficit for the fiscal year that begins in October will be $350 billion. This is a gigantic sum, even for an economy as large as that of the United States.

They do exactly what they prohibit other countries from doing. They say that other countries should not have budget deficits, should not have trade deficits, while they have a trade deficit of about $100 billion. Moreover, the

U.S. budget deficit is a high percentage of the Gross National Product. The IMF and the World Bank do not allow any Latin American country to do the same, to have a budget deficit equal to 7 or 8 percent of its GNP. These agencies, the IMF and the World Bank, insist that it must be 2, 1.5, 1, or 0 percent.

Ten years ago the United States had investments abroad that were $140 billion greater than the investments that other countries had in the United States. In just ten years this positive balance of $140 billion has become a negative balance of $600 billion. That is, foreign investments from other capitalist countries in the United States are now considerably higher than U.S. investments abroad. All these phenomena are completely new, and this is why I was asking where they are going to get the money to help other countries—assuming they really want to help the USSR.

Some Soviet economists, in meetings with Harvard economists, have calculated the foreign aid that would be necessary to develop the market economy in the USSR, and they talk about billions of dollars annually. Where is this money?

These days everyone is asking for money. The Eastern European countries need great quantities of money. The USSR, as some of its economists have stated, needs very large amounts of money; the Middle East needs enormous amounts of money; and Latin America, which owes $430 billion, has paid out $224 billion in the last eight years and needs huge sums of money. No matter how much they talk about neoliberalism and capitalism, where is Latin America going to get the money for its development under these conditions? Instead of receiving money, their participation in world trade becomes less and less, they receive fewer and fewer credits, and they send enormous quantities of money out of the country, much more than they receive.

According to experts, the demand for money in the

world is over $200 billion greater than the supply. There is not enough money to satisfy all the demands: Latin America, the Middle East, the Eastern European countries, the Soviet Union. But the worst thing of all is that the United States needs more money than anyone. Because the question is: Where are they going to get the money to cover the budget deficit of $350 billion they will have next year? Where are they going to get the money to cover the $100 billion trade deficit? The United States has become an octopus, sucking up huge quantities of money, and they themselves need more money than anyone else.

So if Latin America is going to integrate into the U.S. economy, it is going to integrate into the economy of a financially ruined country and it is going to get the worst end of the deal, because what Latin America exports to the United States is principally fuel and raw materials. Sixty percent of what it exports is fuel and raw materials, and less than 30 percent is manufactured products. This is ideal for imperialism: to buy fuel and raw materials cheaply and sell manufactured products at very high prices; and Latin America needs to enter into world trade with manufactured products. These are the kinds of problems and challenges that face the Latin American countries; they are very serious.

You must forgive me if I have gone on about this, because I wanted to give you some idea of the realities in this world.

The famous Uruguay Round—which you must have heard mentioned many times—is not advancing.[23] It consists of a series of negotiations and formulas that have been elaborated to try to promote world trade. And every day there is more protectionism in Europe, more protectionism in Japan and the United States. These protectionist measures are exercised only partially through tariffs. There are many other forms of protectionism: sometimes by establishing impossible requirements for obtaining approval for

"The defeat of the racist army at Cuito Cuanavale has made it possible for me to be here today."

NELSON MANDELA

Fidel Castro greets Nelson Mandela at the Havana airport.

"The blood of the Angolans was our blood, the blood of the Namibians is our blood, and the blood of the South Africans is our blood! Humanity's blood is our blood!"

FIDEL CASTRO

Cuban troops in Angola. (Photos: J. González/*Verde Olivo*)

"Cuito Cuanavale has been a turning point in the struggle to free the continent and our country from the scourge of apartheid!"

NELSON MANDELA

"There can be no greater cause in our era than the one headed by the ANC."

FIDEL CASTRO

Above: celebration of Mandela's release, Johannesburg. Left: meeting sponsored by Transvaal Indian Congress and ANC. Top right: workers on strike near Johannesburg. (Photos from March 1990: Margrethe Siem/*Militant*) Right: delegates to ANC national conference, July 1991. (Photo: Greg McCartan/ *Militant*)

"Ultimately we know that the masses will not only demand but win full rights in a nonracial, nonsexist, democratic South Africa."

NELSON MANDELA

"Your consistent commitment to the systematic eradication of racism is unparalleled." NELSON MANDELA

"The slaves used to do the work here; it is now done by free men and women." FIDEL CASTRO

"Where did injustice come from? Where did inequality come from? Where did poverty come from? Where did underdevelopment come from? Where did all these calamities come from, if not from capitalism?" FIDEL CASTRO

"Imperialism should not sing victory songs. Economically it is weaker than ever." FIDEL CASTRO

Top left: Camagüey, Cuba. (Photo: Joan Campana/*Militant*)
Bottom left: Volunteer construction workers in Havana. (Photo: Cindy Jaquith/*Militant*)
Above: Port-au-Prince, Haiti. (Photo: Tony Savino)

"Our ideas extend beyond all borders. We live in the world that was given to us and we are fighting for a better world, for a world such as that desired by Marx and Engels, where men act as brothers to each other rather than preying on each other like wolves." FIDEL CASTRO

Members of a volunteer construction workers' contingent at International Workers' Day march, Havana, May 1, 1990. (Photo: Jon Hillson/*Militant*)

a product that a Third World country wants to export, sometimes through setting quotas that cannot be exceeded. And apart from all these calamities, the economy of Latin America is threatened by the three great economic blocs and their tendencies to create closed preserves in the economic field. So the peoples of our hemisphere have a very harsh future ahead of them, and that is why it seemed to us an important and historic first step that we gathered together on our own initiative.

We should not create illusions; we should not raise false hopes. This is a very long and difficult process. But the world does not face a very flourishing situation economically. The United States is suffering from the problems I mentioned and more of them; imperialism should not sing victory songs. Militarily the United States is more powerful than ever, and politically it has enormous influence; but economically it is weaker than ever and has very serious problems.

The world will now see how this phenomenon of competition between the great economic blocs evolves, this gigantic demand for capital in the face of limited supply, and it will see how Latin America emerges from its tragedy.

These are the realities that we must be able to analyze calmly, coolly, and objectively, absolutely convinced of the justness of our cause, our ideas, and our plans for confronting problems as serious as those we have before us.

Something curious and unusual has happened today, which is proof that we are not dogmatic: among the thirteen certificates we awarded today, one went to the Sol-Palmeras Hotel, [*Applause*] which we own in partnership with a Spanish firm. We do not have enough capital to develop tourism at the rate we would like, although we are investing quite a bit. Since we have hundreds of kilometers of beaches and extraordinary spots we can accept this kind of joint venture. We rejoice at its success.

We have told the Latin Americans that we are even

willing to give them certain preferential treatment for the sake of integration, for whatever investments they would like to make in Cuba. This would also imply that we have the right to invest in a Latin American country. For example, if we have a specific technology and there are obstacles and barriers, one of the ways of opening markets can be through foreign investments.

With respect to integration with Latin America, we have to adapt our mechanisms to these investment possibilities without renouncing our socialism, because we can easily conceive of economic integration with Latin America without renouncing socialism, even if there are capitalist countries, some going more in that direction and others less. Although there are some that are privatizing even their streets, others are preserving basic industries as public property. Oil, for example, is maintained as an exclusive public resource as well as other specific branches or investments in specific areas. As we told a journalist, no state has to renounce its public property in order to have Latin American integration.

We are ready to seek mutually beneficial and reasonable arrangements with the other Latin American nations, but there is a very important point to remember. We know what we are doing, where our strengths and weaknesses lie, and in what areas we are highly advanced. It would not make sense for us to build a sugar mill, which we can do perfectly well, as a joint venture, or for our sugar enterprises to become joint ventures with foreign interests. What we know how to do and have funds for, we must do ourselves. We can accept foreign capital where we lack the technology, capital, or markets, with greater or lesser amounts of foreign investment. And of course we would give preference to the Latin Americans in this as a necessary phase, or as necessary steps toward economic integration.

We believe that we are the most prepared of anyone for economic integration, and we explained why in the following way: We love our flag a great deal, but if one day it becomes necessary to renounce it in order to form a common nation we will do so. And if one day the world acquires an extraordinary and ideal level of consciousness so that it is able to constitute itself as one great family, we would also be willing to renounce our flag. But we would never do so for the sake of a unipolar world under U.S. imperialist hegemony—this we will never do! We will never renounce a single one of our prerogatives! [*Applause*]

We are internationalists, we are not narrow nationalists or chauvinists. We have shed our blood in other parts of the world, such as in Latin America and Africa. As Mandela recalled, for each person who went on internationalist missions, there were ten who volunteered to go. Is there a more noble people, a people more willing to express their solidarity, a more revolutionary people? The blood of the Angolans was our blood, the blood of the Namibians is our blood, and the blood of the South Africans is our blood! Humanity's blood is our blood! [*Applause*]

Our ideas go beyond chauvinism or narrow nationalism. Our ideas extend beyond all borders. We live in the world that was given to us and we are fighting for a better world. Our minds, our intelligence, and our hearts are prepared for a much better world, for a superior world, for a world such as that desired by Marx and Engels, where men act as brothers to each other rather than preying on each other like wolves.

Capitalism is the greatest creator of wolves in human history, and imperialism has not only been the greatest creator of wolves but also the greatest wolf that has ever existed.

We who come from way back, who were conquered, who were exploited, and who were enslaved throughout history, what marvelous ideas we can defend today; what just ideas we can uphold! And we can think in Latin

American and even world terms.

How far we slaves have come! [*Applause*]

But now internationalism means defending and preserving the Cuban revolution; that is our greatest internationalist duty. [*Applause*] Because when there is a flag like ours, which represents ideas as just as ours, then to defend this trench, this bastion of socialism, is the greatest service we can offer to humanity.

Times are difficult but we will be able to grow and multiply. The 100,000 students who are now participating in agricultural work and other tasks are a proof of our people's spirit, of who our people are and who our youth are. [*Applause*]

Each and every one of us must multiply our efforts. Each worker in his job, each cadre, each party and state official must give all they can of themselves, they must extend themselves, they must be more demanding of themselves and others than ever before. Everyone must rise to this historic moment, and it is well worth doing so! The cause that we defend deserves it so much! Our nation deserves it so much! The ideas that we defend deserve it so much!

Socialism or death!

Patria o muerte! [Homeland or death]

Venceremos! [We will win] [*Ovation*]

RESOLUTION OF THE CUBAN COUNCIL OF STATE

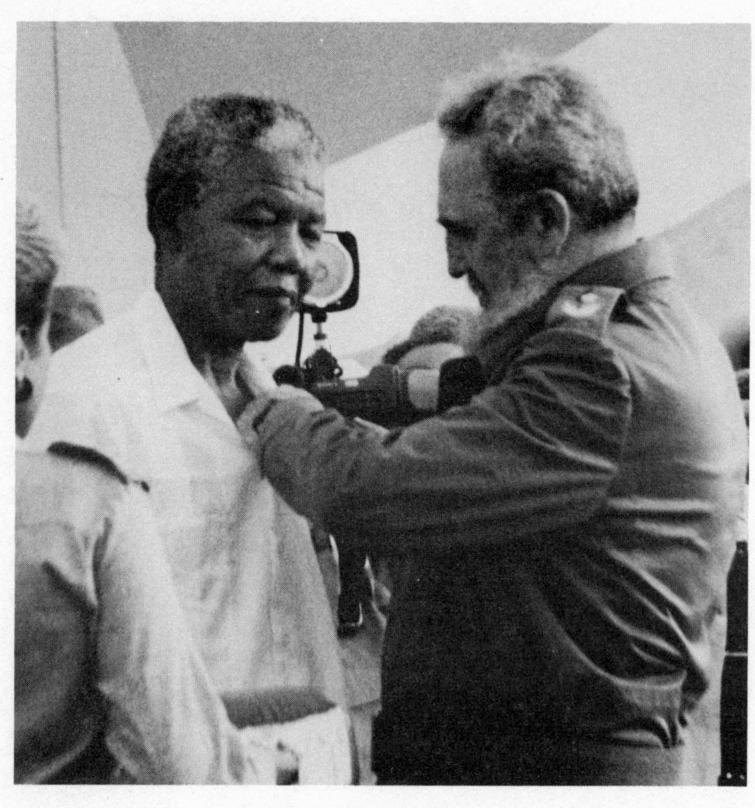

Mandela receives the José Martí award during the July 26 rally. (Photo: Mary-Alice Waters/*Militant*)

RESOLUTION OF THE CUBAN COUNCIL OF STATE

An eloquent testimony of the solidarity between our two peoples

WHEREAS: Nelson Mandela is the highest symbol of the long and heroic struggle of the Black people of South Africa against apartheid and the central leader of the African National Congress, the principal organization that represents the strivings for racial equality and social justice. The ANC is the oldest revolutionary organization on the African continent, and includes in its combative ranks progressive citizens of all races and creeds in the Republic of South Africa. It is leading the battle to create a nonracial, united, and democratic South Africa.

WHEREAS: Our people are honored by the visit to Cuba of one who has dedicated his entire life to the cause of freedom. In 1964, after having been arrested two years previously, Mandela was accused of sabotage and conspiracy to overthrow the government by violent means. Assuming his own defense and that of his comrades in what has become known as the Rivonia trial, the accused became the accuser and denounced with singular courage—even under the threat of death—the crimes of the apartheid regime.

WHEREAS: On a number of occasions during the twenty-seven years of his captivity the outstanding leader of the ANC was offered his freedom in exchange for concessions;

nevertheless, he preferred to remain in prison rather than give in. This stance inspired universal admiration by the peoples of the world, and led to the most powerful clamor in history for the freedom of a prisoner.

WHEREAS: The combination of the revolutionary intransigence of Mandela, the growing struggle of his people, world solidarity, and the military defeat of the South African troops in southern Angola—above all in the battle of Cuito Cuanavale—finally caused the bars of his prolonged captivity to be flung open and initiated the irreversible process of dismantling apartheid.

WHEREAS: Mandela today, at the head of the ANC, is leading this process toward final victory with wise political guidance and firmness of principle. There are still many obstacles along the road to victory, and the people are paying their daily quota of blood, victims of those who finance and organize the wave of violence against the Black population.

WHEREAS: In this decisive hour when the Cuban people have resolved to defend at all costs the revolution, socialism, and the homeland, we take as an example of determination, of struggle, and of faith in victory the heroic stance and tremendous courage of Nelson Mandela, a steadfast combatant and a representative of Africa's best and highest values.

WHEREAS: His presence at this crucial hour not only honors our country but constitutes eloquent testimony of the solidarity between our two peoples, sealed forever with the blood spilled in southern Africa in the common struggle for freedom.

WHEREAS: José Martí, the National Hero of Cuba, was imprisoned by the colonial power when he was barely sixteen years of age and remained steadfast. The shackles that chained him left their painful mark on him for the rest of his life.

WHEREAS: In the foundations of the independent and sovereign republic that he conceived, Martí imparted a humanistic view that excluded all manifestations of racism. He also paid tribute to the men who were brought from Africa and enslaved in Cuba and exalted the national unity that was forged in the crucible of the wars for independence.

BE IT RESOLVED: That the Council of State of the Republic of Cuba, in exercise of the powers conferred upon it, has approved the following RESOLUTION 1695:

FIRST: To grant the José Martí award to the president of the African National Congress NELSON MANDELA on the occasion of his official visit to our country, in recognition of his unyielding stance in the struggle against apartheid and all forms of subjugation and in favor of a united, democratic, and nonracial South Africa.

SECOND: That the medal be officially awarded him by the president of the Council of State, Commander in Chief Fidel Castro Ruz, at the main rally to commemorate the thirty-eighth anniversary of the Moncada assault.

APPROVED in the Palace of the Revolution, Havana, July 25, 1991.

Fidel Castro Ruz
President of the
Council of State

Nelson Mandela

Born in 1918, Nelson Mandela joined the African National Congress in 1944. Together with Walter Sisulu, Oliver Tambo, and others, he helped form the ANC Youth League and was elected its general secretary.

In 1952 Mandela was arrested and received a nine-month suspended sentence for his role as central organizer of the mass Defiance Campaign, in which thousands defied the apartheid regime's internal passport laws and other measures. That same year he was elected ANC deputy national president. In 1956 Mandela and 155 others were arrested on charges of high treason; after five years the defendants were acquitted.

Mandela continued his antiapartheid activities after the ANC's banning in 1960 and was forced to cease public activity in April 1961. That year he helped found Umkhonto we Sizwe (Spear of the Nation) to organize military training and armed operations against the apartheid regime.

In August 1962 Mandela was arrested. Charged with incitement to strike and leaving the country without a passport, he was convicted and sentenced to five years' imprisonment. After other ANC leaders were arrested at Rivonia in 1963, Mandela—already in prison—was tried for sabotage. He was convicted and sentenced to life imprisonment along with seven others.

Held at the notorious Robben Island prison until 1982, Mandela was then transferred to Pollsmoor and later Victor Verster Prison. After refusing Pretoria's offers for his conditional release, he was released without conditions on February 11, 1990.

Elected ANC deputy president shortly after his release, Mandela was chosen the organization's president at the ANC's 1991 congress.

Fidel Castro

Born in eastern Cuba in 1926, Fidel Castro began his political activity while attending the University of Havana in the mid-1940s.

After Fulgencio Batista's coup d'état of March 10, 1952, Castro organized a revolutionary movement to initiate armed struggle against the U.S.-backed dictatorship. On July 26, 1953, he led an unsuccessful attack on the Moncada army garrison in Santiago de Cuba. Many participants were captured and murdered in cold blood; Castro and other survivors were imprisoned. Originally sentenced to fifteen years, he was released in 1955 together with his comrades as a result of an amnesty campaign. Following his release, the July 26 Movement was formed.

In July 1955 Castro left Cuba for Mexico, where he organized a guerrilla expedition to return to Cuba. On December 2, 1956, along with eighty-one other fighters, he landed in southeastern Cuba aboard the yacht *Granma*. For the next two years, Castro directed the operations of the Rebel Army and its expanding network of mass popular support from a base in the Sierra Maestra mountains. On January 1, 1959, Batista was forced to flee Cuba and shortly thereafter Rebel Army units entered Havana.

In February 1959 Castro became prime minister, a position he held until December 1976, when he became president of the Council of State and Council of Ministers. He has been commander in chief of Cuba's armed forces since 1959 and is first secretary of the Central Committee of the Communist Party of Cuba.

1. On July 26, 1953, Fidel Castro led an attack on the Moncada army garrison in Santiago de Cuba, which marked the beginning of the revolutionary struggle against the U.S.-backed tyranny of Fulgencio Batista. After the attack's failure, Batista's forces massacred more than fifty of the captured revolutionaries. Castro and others were taken prisoner, tried, and sentenced to prison. They were released in May 1955 after a public defense campaign forced Batista's regime to issue an amnesty.

On December 2, 1956, eighty-two revolutionary combatants led by Castro landed in southeastern Cuba on the boat *Granma*, following a seven-day journey from Mexico. Despite initial setbacks, the guerrilla fighters were able to establish a base for the Rebel Army in the Sierra Maestra mountains, from which they led the workers and peasants in the revolutionary war against the dictatorship.

On January 1, 1959, in the face of the Rebel Army's advances, Batista fled the country and the revolution triumphed amid a general strike and massive popular mobilizations.

2. Mandela was in Cuba as part of a tour of Latin America and the Caribbean. He also visited Jamaica, Mexico, Venezuela, and Brazil.

3. Earlier at the July 26 rally, Mandela had been awarded the José Martí medal. A noted poet and writer, José Martí founded the Cuban Revolutionary Party in 1892, launched the country's final independence war in 1895, and was killed in battle. The medal that bears Martí's name is the highest honor awarded by Cuba's Council of State.

4. Ernesto Che Guevara, born in Argentina, was a central leader of the Cuban revolution. A guerrilla commander in the revolutionary war, he held leading responsibilities in the new revolutionary government, including as head of the National Bank and minister of industry. In 1965 Guevara resigned his government posts and left Cuba to participate directly in revolutionary struggles in other countries. He spent a number of months in the Congo (today Zaire), where he aided supporters of murdered prime minister Patrice Lumumba in their battle

against the reactionary regime and mercenaries organized and armed by Belgian and U.S. imperialism. Later Guevara went to Bolivia to lead a guerrilla movement against the military dictatorship there. He was captured and killed by the Bolivian army in a CIA-directed operation in 1967.

5. Shortly before Angola's independence from Portuguese colonial rule was to be formally celebrated on November 11, 1975, the country's new government—led by the Popular Movement for the Liberation of Angola (MPLA)—was attacked by South African and Zairean troops. The invading forces were allied with the Angolan National Liberation Front (FNLA) and the Union for the Total Independence of Angola (UNITA).

6. The 1913 Natives Land Act reserved for white ownership the vast majority of the land in South Africa. It was used to drive 3.5 million African farmers off the land and effectively deny them the right to farm.

7. The Freedom Charter was adopted in 1955 by the Congress of the People, a gathering of nearly three thousand delegates held in Kliptown, near Johannesburg. The meeting was convened by the ANC together with the South African Indian Congress, the Coloured People's Organisation, and the Congress of Democrats. The Freedom Charter has served for decades as a guide to action in the battle to bring down apartheid. It is contained in Nelson Mandela, *The Struggle Is My Life*, 2d. ed., (New York: Pathfinder, 1990) and *Nelson Mandela: Speeches 1990* (New York: Pathfinder, 1990).

8. Inkatha, based in Natal Province, is an organization led by KwaZulu Bantustan Chief Minister Mangosuthu Gatsha Buthelezi.

9. Just one week before this speech, it was revealed in the South African press that the apartheid government had secretly funded Inkatha and fomented armed attacks on anti-apartheid activities in an attempt to undercut mass support for the ANC.

10. The National Party, currently led by President F.W. de Klerk, has been the ruling party in South Africa since 1948 and was the architect of the apartheid system.

11. The U.S. government imposed an economic, commercial, and financial embargo on Cuba in the early 1960s.

12. To deal with the economic shortages and disruptions brought about by a sharp reduction in the amount of trade and by new trading terms with the Soviet Union and Eastern Europe, Cuba's National Assembly adopted a major food program in December 1990. At the heart of the program is the mobilization of thousands of Cubans in volunteer work brigades and contingents to meet the labor shortage in agriculture and to help create the conditions for self-sufficiency in food production.

13. The "special period" instituted in 1990 refers to a program of measures designed to help Cuba adjust in an organized way to the consequences of the sharp reduction in trade with the Soviet Union and Eastern Europe. These measures include substantial cutbacks in fuel consumption, a halt to most new construction of housing and social projects, especially in the cities, and the extension of rationing to almost all consumer goods, together with a reduction of the quantities available. The goal of the special program is to equalize the burden of the cutbacks as much as possible while giving priority in the allocation of available resources to food production and economic activities that generate hard currency to pay for needed imports.

14. Earlier at the July 26 rally, the workers at thirteen enterprises were awarded certificates of recognition for their contributions to the social and economic development of Matanzas Province.

Beginning in 1987 special large-scale volunteer construction contingents have been organized to take on major civil-engineering projects such as roads, dams, and other construction work.

15. The Pan American Games were held in Cuba August 2-18, 1991.

16. Mario Muñoz (1912-1953) was one of the revolutionary combatants who participated in the attack on the Moncada garrison. He was captured and murdered by the dictatorship's troops.

17. Nicolás Guillén (1902-1989) was one of Cuba's leading poets.

18. Following the conclusion of the war over colonies between

the U.S. and Spanish governments in 1898, U.S. troops occupied Cuba and helped install a pro-U.S. neocolonial regime. *Mambí* was the Cuban name for that country's independence fighters during Cuba's three wars of independence from Spain during the period 1868-98.

19. Antonio Maceo (1845-1896), José Martí (1853-1895), Máximo Gómez (1836-1905), and Ignacio Agramonte (1841-1873) were leaders of Cuba's independence struggle from Spain during the late nineteenth century. Che Guevara (1928-1967), Camilo Cienfuegos (1932-1959), Abel Santamaría (1927-1953), and Frank País (1934-1957) were leaders of the struggle against the Batista dictatorship that culminated in the victory of the Cuban revolution on January 1, 1959.

20. The First Ibero-American Summit was held in Guadalajara, Mexico, July 17-19, 1991. The event was attended by the heads of state from the Spanish- and Portuguese-speaking countries of Latin America and the Caribbean, plus Spain and Portugal. This was the first time that Cuba had been invited to participate in a gathering of Latin American heads of state since Cuba's expulsion from the Organization of American States in 1962 at the instigation of Washington. Castro headed Cuba's delegation to the meeting.

21. One of the most important measures of the Cuban revolution was the agrarian reform law of 1959, which granted sharecroppers, tenant farmers, and squatters deeds to use of the land they tilled, and set a limit of 1,000 acres on individual holdings. Implementation of this law resulted in the confiscation of the vast estates and sugar plantations in Cuba—many of them owned by U.S. companies; this land passed into the hands of the new government. A second agrarian reform law in 1963 set a maximum limit on holdings of 167 acres.

22. Simón Bolívar (1783-1830) led the armed rebellion that helped win independence from Spain for much of Latin America.

23. This is a reference to the Uruguay Round of the General Agreement on Tariffs and Trade (GATT). Like the International Monetary Fund and World Bank, GATT is one of the international institutions that was created at the initiative of the U.S. capitalist class following its victory in the Second World War in order to help maintain its dominant industrial

and trading position vis-à-vis its imperialist rivals, and to enforce imperialist domination over the colonial and semicolonial world.

The Uruguay Round, which began in 1986, had originally been scheduled to end in December 1990. However, the talks broke down without an agreement being reached and were suspended.

INDEX

FIDEL CASTRO
SPEECHES & INTERVIEWS

To Speak the Truth

by Fidel Castro and Che Guevara

The two central leaders of the Cuban revolution explain to the world why the U.S. government is determined to destroy the example set by that revolution, and why this effort will fail. With an introduction by Mary-Alice Waters. 232 pp., $16.95

In Defense of Socialism

Not only is economic and social progress possible without the dog-eat-dog competition of capitalism, but socialism is the only way forward for humanity. Castro also discusses Cuba's role in advancing the struggle against apartheid in Africa. 142 pp., $13.95

Selected Speeches of Fidel Castro

Speeches from the 1960s and 1970s recounting important chapters in the Cuban revolution. New edition includes Castro's 1961 speech, "I Shall Be a Marxist-Leninist to the End of My Life," explaining why only a socialist revolution can bring about the changes working people are fighting for. $14.00

U.S. Hands Off the Mideast! (1991), $10.95 (Also available in Spanish)

Second Declaration of Havana (1962), $3.00

Cuba Will Never Adopt Capitalist Methods (1988), $3.00

War and Crisis in the Americas (1984-85), $17.95

Nothing Can Stop the Course of History (1985), $18.95

Cuba's Internationalist Foreign Policy (1975-80), $20.95

Building Socialism in Cuba (1960-1982), $20.95

History Will Absolve Me (1953) Together with *Fidel Castro's Political Strategy* by Marta Harnecker, $13.95

AVAILABLE FROM PATHFINDER

BASIC WORKS OF
CHE GUEVARA

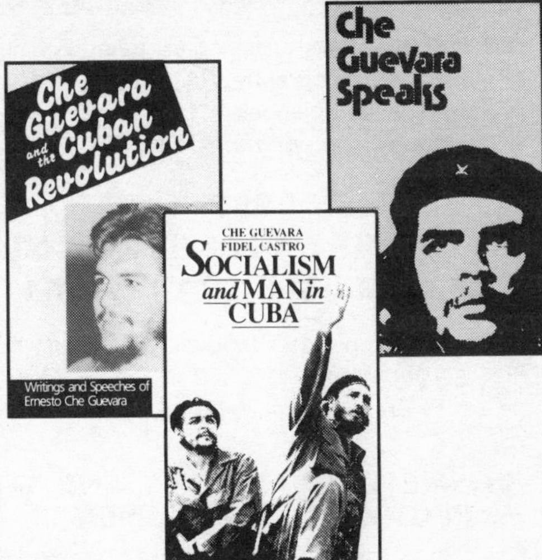

Che Guevara and the Cuban Revolution

WRITINGS AND SPEECHES OF ERNESTO CHE GUEVARA

The most complete collection in English. Discusses the revolutionary war that brought the workers and farmers to victory; Cuba's efforts to overcome economic backwardness; developing a new social consciousness in a society on the road to socialism; and Cuba's commitment to freedom struggles around the world. 413 pp., $21.95

Che Guevara: Economics and Politics in the Transition to Socialism

by Carlos Tablada

Based on Guevara's extensive speeches and writings, explains why building socialism is the task of free men and women transforming themselves and society at the same time. Also available in Spanish and French. 286 pp., $17.95

Socialism and Man in Cuba

by Ernesto Che Guevara and Fidel Castro

Guevara's best-known presentation of the political tasks and challenges in leading the transition from capitalism to socialism. Includes Castro's speech on the 20th anniversary of Guevara's death. Also available in Spanish, French, Farsi, and Swedish. 44 pp., $3.00

Che Guevara Speaks

First published within weeks of Guevara's death in 1967, this collection includes writings and speeches not available elsewhere in English. 159 pp., $12.95

OTHER TITLES FROM PATHFINDER

THE STRUGGLE IS MY LIFE

"My political beliefs have been explained in my autobiography, *The Struggle Is My Life*."
—Nelson Mandela.
by Nelson Mandela, **$15.95**

SPEECHES 1990: INTENSIFY THE STRUGGLE TO ABOLISH APARTHEID

Seven speeches following Mandela's release from prison.
by Nelson Mandela, **$6.00**

COSMETICS, FASHIONS, AND THE EXPLOITATION OF WOMEN

How big business uses women's second-class status to generate profits for a few and perpetuate the oppression of the female sex and the exploitation of working people.
by Joseph Hansen, Evelyn Reed, and Mary-Alice Waters, **$12.95**

THE CHANGING FACE OF U.S. POLITICS
Working-Class Politics and the Trade Unions

Building a revolutionary workers' party in a world of capitalist economic crises, wars, trade conflicts, antiunion assaults, and attacks on workers' rights and individual liberties.
by Jack Barnes, **$19.95**

THOMAS SANKARA SPEAKS

Speeches and writings by the assassinated president of Burkina Faso tell the story of the 1983-87 revolution that unfolded in this West African country as peasants and workers began confronting hunger, illiteracy, the oppression of women, and other conditions perpetuated by capitalism. **$18.95**

THE REVOLUTION BETRAYED
What Is the Soviet Union and Where Is It Going?

The classic study of the degeneration of the revolutionary leadership of the Soviet Union in the 1920s and '30s that explains the roots of the crisis rocking the former Soviet bloc today. (Also available in Spanish.)
by Leon Trotsky, **$19.95**

CHE GUEVARA AND THE FIGHT FOR SOCIALISM TODAY

Cuba Confronts the World Crisis of the '90s

Socialism can be built only by free men and women who consciously work together to lay the foundations for a new society, transforming themselves in the process. That course, which Ernesto Che Guevara championed in the early years of the Cuban revolution, remains central for Cuban working people today as they confront the biggest challenges yet in the history of the revolution. Also available in Spanish and French.
by Mary-Alice Waters, **$3.50**

THE COMMUNIST MANIFESTO

Founding document of the modern revolutionary workers' movement. Explains how capitalism arose as a specific stage in the economic development of class society, and how it will be superseded through the revolutionary action of the international working class.
by Karl Marx and Frederick Engels, **$2.50**

FARMERS FACE THE CRISIS OF THE 1990s

Examines the deepening economic and social crisis in the capitalist world and explains how farmers and workers can unite internationally against the mounting assaults from the billionaire bankers, industrialists, and merchants.
by Doug Jenness, **$3.50**

FEBRUARY 1965: THE FINAL SPEECHES

Speeches from the last three weeks of Malcolm X's life presenting the still accelerating evolution of his political views.
by Malcolm X, **$17.95**

THE EASTERN AIRLINES STRIKE

Accomplishments of the Rank-and-File Machinists

The story of the 22-month strike that defeated the attempt to demonstrate that Eastern's antiunion onslaught was the way to a profitable nonunion airline.
by Ernie Mailhot and others, **$9.95**

WRITE FOR A FREE CATALOG. SEE ADDRESSES AT FRONT OF BOOK.